# The Story of the
# *Daily Worker*

# The Story of the
# *Daily Worker*

## by William Rust

*edited and completed by*
**Allen Hutt**

*with a foreword by*
**J.R. Campbell**

*2010 edition edited by*
**James Eagle**

People's Press Printing Society, London

First published in 1949 by P.P.P.S. Ltd
75 Farringdon Road, London E.C.1

This edition published in 2010 by P.P.P.S Ltd
52 Beachy Road, London E3
www.morningstaronline.co.uk

ISBN: 978-0-9541473-1-0

# Contents

Foreword...............................................................................6

Editor's Note....................................................................10

Editor's Note to the 1949 edition..............................11

Foreword to the 1949 edition......................................12

I        Our First Year.........................................................15

II       Persecution and Growth........................................37

III      The People's Front Against Fascism....................52

IV      We Fought for Spain and Unity...........................71

V        The Year of Munich..............................................95

VI      Nineteen Thirty-nine..........................................118

VII     The War—and Suppression................................151

VIII    The Fight to Beat the Ban..................................175

IX      Back into Action..................................................201

X        The Only Daily Paper owned by its Readers......236

Index...............................................................................264

*Illustrations between pp. 127-142*

# Foreword

I F WILLIAM RUST landed up in 2010 he would not, I suspect, be surprised to find that "that damned paper" is still coming out—although as the *Morning Star* rather than under the name it bore when he founded it 80 years ago. But not much else has worked out how he and his colleagues probably foresaw it when they gathered in an old warehouse in Shoreditch for an experiment which even Rust must have had his doubts about.

Still, they may have been forging ahead with nothing like the financial resources of the existing dailies and in the face of poisonous Establishment hostility—both of which have remained constants down the years—but they were convinced they had history on their side. Mere weeks before, the U.S. stock-market crash had kicked the legs out from under a British economy still struggling to pick itself up after World War I. Who was to say, as depression set in across the world, that capitalism would ever recover? Especially when amidst it all one country, the Soviet Union, was not only untouched but booming?

As late as 1949 Rust's successor as editor, J.R. Campbell, was able to write in his foreword to this book that the common people's "triumph over decaying capitalism cannot long be delayed."

And he doesn't seem overconfident when Nazism had just been smashed thanks chiefly to the Soviet Union's war machine and British voters had just returned the most left-wing government in their history, which promptly set about remaking the country in a new and better mould—and when the *Daily Worker* itself had a new building and machinery, a new cutting-edge design and thousands of new readers. The tide had turned, and who knew how far it would carry the left?

Not much further, as it turned out, and 1949 was not far from the high water mark before the tide turned again and the British left, and the *Daily Worker*, were battered by a stream of defeats, setbacks and rearguard actions. Labour's shock defeat in 1951, Khrushchev's secret speech, the Soviet invasions of Hungary and Czechoslovakia—the *Daily Worker* supported the first and opposed the second, but both cost it many experienced staff and thousands of readers, and disillusioned countless more socialists further afield—then Thatcherism, Wapping, the Miners' Strike, the collapse of the Soviet Union, and a dedicated drive by Tory and Labour to reverse all the greatest achievements of the Attlee government, from British Rail to the National Health Service.

And so it is that our hypothetical Rust would find himself in a 2010 all too hauntingly familiar, right down to the former warehouse in east London from which the *Morning Star* is published these days. Not by candlelight nor with freezing feet, admittedly (and Rust, and his overworked staff, would surely have loved the sleek slabs of plastic and aluminium with which modern newspapers are made). Nor in Shoreditch any more, although the march of shiny office blocks, expensive bars and advertising agencies that have driven out that area's working-class occupants along with their livelihoods would tell Rust volumes about modern Britain and its priorities.

But the building bears William Rust's name above the door and far too much outside has the ring of Rust's era. Stock market crashes and wage cuts, job losses and overseas occupations, right-wing Labour politicians eyeing a coalition with the Liberals to save their skins—and the lurking threat of fascism, although this time with Muslims not Jews as the hate figure of choice.

So Rust wouldn't be surprised to find his paper still coming out. He and his comrades (including this book's original editor, the legendary chief sub Allen Hutt) took seriously Harry Pollitt's declaration that "the paper is born and must never be allowed to die", to the point of running the linotypes by hand, working all night to pump out water during the blitz and setting up an entire distribution network to beat a national wholesalers' boycott—setting the tone for the trials that *Daily Worker* and *Morning Star* staff have endured down the years.

He might wonder what went wrong so that the paper spent most of the intervening decades clinging on desperately in the face of a right-wing backlash rather than, as he might have hoped, becoming the leading daily of a new, socialist Britain. But once he realised how things are Rust would surely call to mind this description of the *Daily Worker's* mission at its birth which, he said, "has also an excellent application in 1949" and in 2010 too—to be "the standard for rallying the working class for the counter-offensive against capitalist rationalisation ... for the fight against speeding-up, wage cuts, overtime and unemployment ... and against the Labour Government of rationalisation ... and preparations for another imperialist war."

This book is a lesson in how Rust and his staff set about that, in its style as well as its content. It tells far more than just the story of the paper, stitching that particular thread into a broad tapestry of world events across two tumultuous decades of war and peace, fascism and resistance, strikes, bans, bombs, scandal and, in the end, hope of a better world. It's a take on history that you won't read in the school textbooks, from a staunchly socialist standpoint but told with verve and punch—big events and complex issues set out simply and clearly, opinions argued with passion and honesty. Rust may, in his first chapter, disclaim any journalistic experience before embarking on this adventure, but he was a born newspaperman. And if he sometimes seems to cling too tenaciously to the party line, that probably stems from the same source as the crackling energy of his writing here, the same energy he brought to the pages of the *Daily Worker*—the energy of someone confident in his cause and his chances of victory. That drive and dedication, in Rust and tens of thousands of others, was what propelled the British left to the high point at which this book was written, when the Establishment was trembling in fear and a new world seemed not only possible, not only necessary—as it still is—but just around the corner.

JAMES EAGLE
Assistant editor, the *Morning Star*

# Editor's Note
## to the 2010 edition

THE TEXT IS as it was published in 1949, except for the correction of a few spelling errors (without, hopefully, introducing too many new ones). Although Rust's style has stood the test of time, many of his cultural assumptions haven't—the likes of Hamilton Fyfe, François Darlan or the notorious J.H. Thomas, brought down by a scandal involving a businessman revelling in the nickname of "Cosher", are no longer the household names they once were and so I have added footnotes where it seems necessary. All other annotations are Rust's and Hutt's own. As well as the original illustrations between pages 127 and 142, I have added various cartoons and articles drawn from the *Daily Worker's* archives. My thanks to the Marx Memorial Library and John Callow in particular for their help in compiling these, and to Mark Howe, whose book *Is That Damned Paper Still Coming Out?* was an invaluable source of information.

J.E.

# Editor's Note
## to the 1949 edition

WHEN WILLIAM RUST died in February 1949 he had written the first six chapters of this book, bringing our story up to the war. The exacting research and writing had been one of the principal spare-time occupations—and how many he had!—of the last months of his life. As each chapter was written I had the opportunity to discuss it with him; on the basis of those discussions, and bearing in mind that he did not have the chance to do any final revision, I have made certain minor emendations in the text which follows.

The last four chapters, which cover the ten years from the outbreak of war to the present day, it has been my great privilege to undertake. Bill left no notes or treatment for this latter period; but after I had drafted the chapter headings a notebook of his was discovered with a list of proposed chapters which were identical with my draft. It goes without saying that I have adhered to his method of relating the paper's history throughout to the political and industrial events of the day. This makes the present work a good deal more than the history of a newspaper and, in my opinion, is its special virtue.

G.A.H.

# Foreword
## to the 1949 edition

IN THE MONTHS previous to his death our late Comrade William Rust was engaged in writing a short history of the *Daily Worker*. His object was to show to the new generation of readers the great role which the *Daily Worker* had played in all the struggles of the working class since 1930 and of the unprecedented sacrifices which made possible the present modern building and plant and up-to-date newspaper.

No one was better qualified for this task. Bill was the Editor of the paper for its first three years of existence and from October, 1939 until his sad death in February, 1949. He knew the paper in the first precarious years of its life when it was to a large extent an excellent hard-hitting propaganda commentary on the previous day's news. These were the years in which the staff lived under the menace of prosecution for sedition and of libel actions. They were the years in which the capitalist press attributed the very existence of the paper to Moscow gold.

As the Editor of the paper during the war years Bill was mainly responsible for the conception of transforming the paper, with its greatly increased popular support, into an up-to-date, modern newspaper, basing itself on the latest technique. In this he had the expert and indispensable advice of Allen Hutt, who came back to the paper as chief sub-editor when it restarted after the lifting of the ban in 1942.

The amount of money raised by the paper since 1942 is astonishing. In the Fighting Fund which meets our monthly deficit and in the share capital subscribed to the People's Press Printing Society we have collected a total sum of £545,450. Nothing like this amount has ever previously been raised for a paper by the voluntary effort of individuals in the British working-class movement. It far surpasses the similar efforts to sustain the *Daily Herald* in the period after the first war and outshines even the collective effort of the Trades Union Congress at the time when that body was responsible for the upkeep of the *Herald*. Few people believed that a sum of this character could be raised by the chief supporters of the *Daily Worker*—the Communist Party and its sympathisers. Bill Rust was one of the few and his faith was justified.

When the paper resumed many of the leading comrades, Fred Pateman, Bill Shepherd, Phil Bolsover, Gabriel, were in the forces. In the Editor, Walter Holmes, Frank Pitcairn, Ivor Montagu, Jack Owen and myself the paper had a plentiful supply of writers. It is always easier to get writers than it is to get an efficient sub-editorial staff. Steady, careful political education for the staff was organised under the control of the Editor while Allen Hutt laboured away at technical instruction. Space in our small wartime paper was very limited and writers and reporters groaned when they saw their brightest efforts reduced to a few paragraphs. However, it did them a world of good.

With the launching of the larger paper on November 1, 1948, it was clear that a new phase of our history had opened. Bill had already felt that it would be worth while writing a short history of the paper for the particular benefit of those readers who had come to us in wartime. So he started in the autumn of 1948 working late into the night and approximately half of the present history had been completed by the time of his death on February 3, 1949.

The whole volume contains a great and inspiring story, which deserves to be in the hands of all who are fighting for peace and for Socialism. It appears at a time when the world capitalist crisis is deepening and when the capitalists and their lackeys in the working-class movement have organised a furious campaign against the Communists. It should inspire everyone to fight back resolutely in the knowledge that the common people have great resources of talent at their disposal and that their triumph over decaying capitalism cannot long be delayed.

J.R. CAMPBELL

# Chapter One
# Our First Year

O N DECEMBER 31, 1929, eight men* gathered in an old warehouse on Tabernacle Street, London, E.C.2, in order to produce the first number of the *Daily Worker,* which had been promised for January 1, 1930. Among them was William Gallacher, who nearly six years later was to be elected Communist M.P. for West Fife. The new paper was the successor of the *Workers' Life,* weekly organ of the Communist Party, which for some months had carried the inscription on its front page—"Forerunner of the *Daily Worker.*"

I had been chosen as editor although it must be said that my experience of daily journalism was practically nil. As a lad I had worked in the offices of the Hulton Press and had seen a little of Fleet Street from the inside; I had also edited the *Young Worker* for the Young Communist League and had written a number of articles and pamphlets. As I told the Press Commission when I

...............................

\* In fact there were eight men and one woman—Kay Beauchamp, the paper's first women's editor, was working alongside Rust, Gallacher, Walter Holmes, R. Page Arnot, Frank Paterson, W.G. Shepherd, Brennan Ward and Tom Wintringham.—J.E.

appeared before them in February, 1948, I was pitchforked into the job. It was my reward, I suppose, for my somewhat persistent advocacy of the importance of a Communist daily in Britain.

With the exception of Allen Hutt, who joined us three months after our start, and Walter Holmes, both of whom had worked on the *Daily Herald,* not one of us had previous experience on a daily newspaper. But what we lacked in experience we substituted for in enthusiasm, courage and political conviction. I would be the last to discount the importance of journalistic training and command of technique as to do so would be to disregard all that my years on the *Daily Worker* has taught me. But the launching of the *Daily Worker* in 1930 was a political decision, it arose out of the necessities of the situation and it could not wait interminably on the gathering of a staff which possessed both journalistic experience and political understanding. In any case, such persons were few and far between in those days.

The publication of the *Daily Worker* on January 1, 1930, was a political event as was demonstrated by the reception accorded to it by the Government and the other newspapers, particularly *The Times.* It should also be remembered that the *Daily Worker* was the fruit of a political fight within the ranks of the Communist Party, a long drawn-out conflict on whether the establishment of a Communist daily newspaper under British conditions was really possible. In the end the doubters and the pessimists were routed.

It must be conceded, however, that these doubters had some logic on their side. The capitalist Press in Britain is a great monopoly concern and its successful finances are based on vast circulations and the huge advertising revenues which these circulations bring. Dealing with the problem of starting new papers, Wickham Steed, former editor of *The Times*, once wrote that the entrance fee to the world of Press monopoly was not less than £2,000,000. And the *Daily Herald*, which passed over to Odhams during the same year that marked the birth of the *Daily Worker*, certainly paid an entrance fee of that size. The costs of the capitalisation of the Odhams' *Herald* were so fantastic that it was ten years before it began to make a profit even though it reached a circulation of two millions.

The failure of the Labour movement to maintain its own daily newspaper and the financial collapse of the *Daily Chronicle* at a time when it had a circulation of 900,000, were certainly not good auguries for the success of the new Communist daily which had to be launched without financial resources. Our critics were convinced that the *Daily Worker* was a Mad Hatter scheme, and we were somewhat amused and not in the least surprised when the *Daily Herald* rang us up on the first day of our appearance to know if it were true that the *Daily Worker* was not coming out again. They were told to their great disappointment that the *Daily Worker* had come to stop. But although we answered so confidently we knew little then of the difficulties and hardships that were to confront us and the ferocity of the attack we were to encounter.

It is no exaggeration to assert that the members of the Communist Party and the militant section of the Labour movement were greatly inspired by the appearance of the long-awaited and long-discussed paper. It had many crudities and it was hastily slung together. But it was there and all supporters felt that it was a triumph for the revolutionary idea and that time and experience would bring about the necessary improvements in its contents.

The appearance of the *Daily Worker* marked the beginning of a transformation in the work of the Communist Party which now had at its disposal a daily weapon for the advancement of its agitation and propaganda. It meant that the Communist Party was now able to advance from the stage of general propaganda to the handling of daily political events as they occurred, to give a daily and direct answer to the problems before the people as they arose and to organise action in support of its policy.

"Without a political organ, a movement deserving to be called a political movement is impossible in modern Europe," wrote Lenin; and this quotation was prominently displayed in our first number. It is worth recalling that Lenin always attached the greatest importance to the establishment of a daily newspaper in Britain be it ever so small or limited in its circulation.

In his famous letter to Tom Bell, written in 1921, Lenin discussed the possibilities of starting a daily paper of the working class, even in the form of "small leaflets daily as a beginning of the really proletarian Communist newspaper," and even if limited for the time being to South Wales, where the miners' union had passed a resolution in support of the Communist International. "You must start this paper," he wrote, "not as a business (as usually papers are started in capitalist countries)—not with a big sum of money, not in the ordinary and usual manner—but as an *economic & political* tool of the *masses* in their struggle." Finally, he warned that the "English Government will apply the shrewdest means in order to suppress every beginning of this kind." Nine years after these words were written we were to experience the grim seriousness of their meaning.

The first number of the *Daily Worker* was closely scrutinised in Fleet Street and attention was immediately centred on the message we published from the Presidium of the Communist International greeting the appearance of the new paper, which it described as "the standard for rallying the working class for the counter-offensive against capitalist rationalisation. It will be the rallying point for the fight against speeding-up, wage cuts, overtime and unemployment; against the suppression of strikes and arbitration, and against the Labour Government of rationalisation, anti-Soviet intrigues, colonial brutalities and preparations for another imperialist war." One may say in passing that this description of the tasks of the *Daily Worker* in 1930 has also an excellent application in 1949.

This message served as a pretext for an attack on the *Daily Worker* and the Soviet Government which *The Times* launched in a furious leading article the following day and which in the ensuing weeks was taken up by other newspapers and reactionary Members of Parliament. Our appearance had certainly caused a sensation and we had stepped right into the centre of the political scene. *The Times* wrote as follows:

"A Communist daily newspaper, which began its existence in London yesterday, publishes a message from the Presidium of the Communist International, which is a flagrant piece of Bolshevik propaganda. The message is directed mainly against the Labour Government and against the trade union leaders. Mr. Henderson has assured the House of Commons that the Government will insist on the observance of the Soviet pledge which is clearly applicable to the propaganda activities of the Comintern. Now we have the Comintern's reply to Mr Henderson. It is now his turn to act, and with a directness that will prevent all misunderstanding in Moscow."

In later years, during the period of the common fight against Hitler Fascism, *The Times,* which in 1930 had expressed its alarm at our appearance, was itself denounced as being nothing more or less than a "threepenny edition of the *Daily Worker*" by a Conservative M.P. But the *Daily Worker,* I am happy to say, has never been described as a penny edition of *The Times.*

During the 'thirties it was one of the favourite propaganda stunts of the Labour and Conservative parties to attribute the activities of the Communist International to the Soviet Government and to wax indignant about this interference in British affairs by a foreign government just as the Press in these days denounces the Information Bureau of the Communist Parties as an instrument of Moscow.

Now the pack was in full cry and they kept it fiercely up until Mr. Arthur Henderson, the Foreign Secretary, made the

announcement on January 22 that he had informed the Soviet
Ambassador that the message of the Communist International
was "calculated to impede relations between the two countries."
But by May, Fleet Street was at it again and the Tories in the
House of Commons succeeded in extracting an answer from Mr.
Henderson that the question of the *Daily Worker* was receiving
"serious consideration," and a comment by his Under-Secretary,
Mr. Hugh Dalton, about the "obviously serious nature" of cer-
tain statements we had made. Prominent in this questioning was
Mr. Smithers, the Member for Chislehurst, who has now become
notorious as Sir Waldron, the Tories' Cave Man No. 1.

Foremost in the hunt was the *Morning Post,* that ultra-Tory
sheet which we have succeeded in outliving. It had to be igno-
miniously wound up in 1937 as it could not pay its way and
the wealthy Tories who backed it did not love it sufficiently to
start a fighting fund. On May 22, 1930, the *Morning Post* wrote
that: "The *Daily Worker,* by its flat defiance, shows that it is not
afraid of the Government, but the Government are afraid of the
*Daily Worker....* What repercussion is such a pitiable exhibition
of weakness likely to have in India, even if the incitements to
mutiny are ineffective in the Army."

This was the reply of the *Morning Post* to appeals by the *Daily
Worker* that workers should not handle munitions for India
and that soldiers should stand by their class. The *Post* also sent
a special correspondent down to Aldershot to disprove a *Daily
Worker* report about bad living conditions for the soldiers. He
reported that there were no complaints except about the golden

pudding! Following this effort the *Morning Post* sent a reporter to the *Daily Worker* office to ask if I had been arrested yet. For several days the *Morning Post* continued to kick up a great fuss about the *Daily Worker* leading article which had commended the action of Indian troops who had handed over their rifles to insurgents. This article was described as "rank sedition."

But the *Morning Post* was to learn that there are more ways of killing a cat than choking it with cream. The day after Mr. Henderson made his statement in the House, the Federation of London Wholesale Newsagents moved into action against the *Daily Worker*. They announced their intention not to handle the *Daily Worker* in future. This decision in fact completed the national boycott of the *Daily Worker* by the wholesalers.

As early as January 24 the big Lancashire wholesalers had suddenly cancelled all orders without warning. The Provincial Federation followed suit two days later. London firms held their hand until May. Scotland followed in July. A few of the smaller wholesalers continued to co-operate but this general boycott was maintained for a period of twelve years, until the *Daily Worker* was republished in September, 1942, following the lifting of the ban imposed in January, 1941.

This boycott was, of course, a real body blow against the *Daily Worker*. All newspapers in Britain are distributed by wholesalers who collect from the newspaper offices or railway stations and deliver the papers direct to the vast network of newsagents numbering about 50,000. The boycott meant that the *Daily Worker* had to improvise its own distribution machinery and in the provinces to collect from the railway stations and to see that the papers were taken to the various newsagents.

Such a boycott, which undoubtedly the wholesalers had no right in law to impose, might well have broken any other paper. But the *Daily Worker* took up the challenge and fought back. Speaking at a London conference in reply to the first ban in January, Harry Pollitt declared that "the paper is born and must never be allowed to die. If we keep that fixed in our minds we shall be invincible."

The story of the battle against the wholesalers' boycott is one of the most inspiring in the history of the *Daily Worker*. The challenge was taken up and throughout the country our energetic supporters were to be found in the small hours of the morning collecting parcels at the railway stations and delivering them to newsagents or direct to readers. The sale of the *Daily Worker* on the evening before publication became a familiar sight in the streets of London. It was a great test and the paper came through with flying colours.

The setting up of this independent distribution machinery was a heavy strain on the limited funds of the *Daily Worker* and the energies of its readers but it may truly be said that the wholesalers defeated their own purpose. Close, unbreakable ties were established between the paper and its readers, the selling of the *Daily Worker* became a regular task of the Communist Party and great public interest and sympathy was aroused in the fight of a gallant little paper which was beset on all sides.

Special mention must here be made of the co-operative attitude of the great majority of the newsagents who had no interest in the wholesalers' boycott and who continued to sell the paper as in the past. The Retailers' Federation made it quite clear that they were in favour of giving the *Daily Worker* a fair crack of the whip. This attitude of the newsagents has always been deeply appreciated by the staff of the *Daily Worker* and we are more than grateful for their valuable help; it marks the political difference between the attitude of big business and small business.

In the following year, the organ of the newsagents, *The Newsagent and Booksellers' World,* wrote:

"Publishers and wholesalers have banned the *Daily Worker* for reasons best known to themselves. Retailers will handle where they can get it but it is not very easy. It would, however, be of some little interest to the *World's* readers to learn that the paper still lives. It has a fairly good circulation, and last week managed to increase it by about 12,000 copies. In comparison with the great national dailies the circulation is insignificant. Nevertheless, bearing in mind that the paper has to resort to unorthodox methods to secure circulation, it is a triumph of newspaper production."

"A triumph of newspaper production." Those words were often to be repeated in the years ahead.

During these early years of the *Daily Worker* we did not own the printing plant where the paper was produced but entered into a contract with the Utopia Press, Ltd., which possessed an old German rotary machine that had been installed as long ago as 1914 for the printing of Robert Blatchford's *Clarion*. It was a purely business arrangement which the proprietor of the printing works, Mr. W.T. Wilkinson, an old and somewhat nervous gentleman, entered into solely on the grounds of its profitability. His works were in Worship Street and a couple of hundred yards from our editorial and business offices in Tabernacle Street, so that editorial copy had to be taken round by boys with sometimes disastrous consequences. I well remember the occasion when one of our bright lads got engaged in a game of football on his way to Worship Street and returned in tears to our office to announce that he had lost the front page "splash."

Our offices were a rather grim, not say grimy, affair, and owing to various obstacles it took quite a time settling in. The ground landlords were the Ecclesiastical Commissioners and, as they were not particularly co-operative, negotiations for the lease dragged heavily with the result that we were unable to effect the necessary technical preparations. On the night of publication we were working without light, heat, telephones or tape machines. What could we do? We had promised the *Daily Worker* for January 1 and the promise had to be honoured. In our issue of January 4, in an article entitled "By Candlelight in an Old Grimy Warehouse," I told our readers the story of this extraordinary beginning. "Working by candlelight and with freezing feet we got out the first working-class daily in Britain," I wrote. "Although the office is cold, the *Daily Worker* and the workers around us are afire with the invincible revolutionary spirit of the working class."

Our editions were, I am afraid, very late and we lost trains. But we were out and that was all that mattered at that moment. We were then giving our readers twelve small pages with no photographs and practically no advertisements. It should be remembered that the other popular nationals were then publishing twenty to twenty-four lavishly illustrated large pages a day and running crazy circulation campaigns for which they employed small armies of canvassers who offered would-be readers all kinds of inducements including books, cameras and household goods. Even gold wristlet watches were offered. This campaign, which was estimated to have cost Fleet Street over £3,000,000, reached its highest point in the period 1931-33.

Messrs. Odhams, in their efforts to boost up the circulation of the newly-acquired *Daily Herald,* were the pacemakers of these methods of obtaining readers even before the *Herald* was transferred to Long Acre in March, 1930. As early as January 8, we published a report of a *Daily Herald* Regional Conference where members of the Labour movement were offered money bribes of 9d. for every new reader. An additional 6d. was to be paid to the canvasser's trade union or local Labour Party. The same day we published a report that the Guildford Labour Party had declined to be represented at one of these regional conferences on the grounds that the *Daily Herald* was now a capitalist newspaper. It is stated in the P.E.P. Report on the British Press that the raising of the circulation of the *Daily Herald* from 400,000 to 1,750,000 cost £1,325,000, or £1 per head.

Our circulation-pushing was confined to the voluntary efforts of our supporters and all we could offer them was honourable mention in the paper in return for their efforts. Money was always tight with us and always will be, I suppose. For one thing, the advertisers would not touch us with a barge pole and many years were to pass before we succeeded in establishing ourselves in that field.

Advertisements, it should be remembered, are financially the life's blood of the British Press. Both the cheap, popular papers and the so-called quality journals are dependent on advertising revenue as all newspapers are sold below the costs of production. Such is the method of newspaper production which has been established in Britain over a long period of years and which is more or less accepted as a natural state of affairs. This results in various forms of corruption and the exercise by some advertisers of an influence over the publication of editorial matter.

But this is by no means the most serious feature of the powerful position occupied by the advertisers in relation to the Press. This method of newspaper finance means that the big newspapers, in themselves monopoly capitalist institutions, are closely tied to the capitalist system as a whole and that their news presentation is necessarily coloured from the upper-class standpoint. It also shows the utter impracticability of schemes for the democratic control of the Press from the outside. To establish democratic control of the Press it will first be necessary to have a revolution in Fleet Street and to end the dominating power of the advertisers, i.e., the big capitalist firms and banks.

Giving evidence later to the Royal Commission on the Press,

Mr. Francis Williams, a former editor of the *Daily Herald,* said that leading articles in his paper were altered by the commercial proprietors without consultation and there were numerous occasions when they deleted material on the grounds that a too vigorous presentation of the policy of the Labour movement might drive away some advertising support.

In his book on *Press, Parliament and People,* Mr. Williams complains of the influence exerted by his managing director, the late Lord Southwood. "Editorially the *Daily Herald* was under constant compulsion to be bright.... He (Lord Southwood) did not at that time display much interest in what they said; it was how they looked that affected him. He judged a newspaper by how it attracted the popular eye; did it look bright, cheerful, entertaining, exciting; would it make people optimistic?"

Optimism gratifies the advertisers and keeps readers' minds off the nasty realities of the capitalist system. The pursuit of optimism in the form of bright news and items of entertainment and distraction is an automatic part of the Press lords' approach. It not only degrades journalism and popular taste, but also facilitates the putting over of pernicious political propaganda. The *Daily Express* front page slogan in 1939—"There Will Be No War"—might be disguised as optimistic stupidity, but it was none the less most harmful and dangerous. Much of the optimism in the Press in those months was, however, by no means a reflection of stupidity, but the result of propaganda work carefully organised by Sir Samuel Hoare (Lord Templewood), who was then Foreign Secretary. Mr. Francis Williams tells the story of how Hoare arranged confidential conferences with proprietors and editors; the mild reception given by the Cabinet to the German demand that no news or opinions unwelcome to Hitler should appear in the British Press; and how Chamberlain gave out a confidential everything-in-the-garden-is-lovely story just a few days before the invasion of Czechoslovakia.

The year of our birth was mighty tough going but we managed to pull through despite our acute financial difficulties. We had begun with hardly any capital and we had to set our Fighting Fund, which was to cover the deficit on production, at £300 a month. The Fund actually realised in 1930 no less than £5,000. Many were the suggestions in Press and Parliament that the *Daily Worker* was in receipt of lavish supplies of Moscow gold but the daily scrapings in Tabernacle Street to make both ends meet were sufficient answer to this baseless propaganda story.

Up to April we kept the paper at twelve small pages; then on May 1 we went to double the size with six pages; this format we maintained until June, 1940, when the exigencies of newsprint rationing drove us back to the little paper again. The May Day number marked a considerable improvement in make-up and the leading article was transferred to page one. Later it got back inside again but it is now firmly established outside. This innovation—at least for the British Press—has been followed in recent years by the *Daily Mail* and the *Daily Graphic.* The *Daily Mirror,* which now has its leader on the back page, also seems to be moving in that direction. It was therefore rather nasty of *The Economist,* when we went over to our enlarged paper on November 1, 1948, to suggest that our front page make-up closely resembled the *Daily Mail!*

On April 1 we introduced the "Worker's Notebook," which became one of our most popular and pungent features and with which the name of Walter Holmes will always be associated. It was preceded by a similar feature, entitled "Bread and Cheese," which was largely written by William Gallacher. Cartoons in those days were few and far between. Our first cartoonist, Maro, did not join us until 1933; the famous Gabriel not until three years later. "Bejay,"* the talented humorous writer, began with us in October, 1930. He is now "Yaffle" of *Reynolds News.*

Sport, I regret to say, received very short shrift in our paper as it was dropped after only three weeks on the grounds that it was a sink of corruption and a means of doping the working class. In those days we were more than a little sectarian! The tipster I had engaged therefore had to go. I think he was a better politician than a tipster and he made various endeavours to persuade me to permit him to sign his racing notes as "Nilats"—on the grounds that it was Stalin backwards. Five years were to elapse before sport was restored to its rightful place in our columns. Today we have a first-class sports staff. "Cayton" on horse racing and A.A. Thomas on cricket have really made their mark. Our football and cricket annuals enjoy a very wide sale.

From time to time, the *Daily Worker* offices were hungrily

......................................................

* Basil Boothroyd, who would go on to have a long career in TV and radio including decades as a humorous writer for *Punch.*—J.E.

watched by the police, if only for the purpose of noting who went in and out, in order that the "splits" could familiarise themselves with the faces of our staff. We would occasionally draw the attention of our readers to this practice and make appropriate comments. Ordinarily-dressed detectives were not always used on this job. Sometimes the spying was done by roughly-dressed coppers of unshaven appearance.

But it was not until July, 1930, that our first serious brush with the authorities took place and the *Daily Worker* found itself in the dock at the High Court of Justice charged with contempt of court and lowering the authority of Mr. Justice Rigby Swift. Our business manager, Frank Priestley, was sentenced to nine months' imprisonment; two of the partners of the Workers' Press, the company responsible for publishing the paper, were also sentenced. Frank Paterson, who is still with us in the Advertisement Department, got six months and F. Brennan Ward got five months. Our printer, Mr W.T. Wilkinson, was ordered to pay a fine of £250 and £25 towards the cost of the proceedings. He had tendered an apology and had intimated that he would consider ending his contract with the *Daily Worker*. The third partner of the Workers' Press, R. McIlhone, did not put in an appearance and remained free until January, 1931, when he was sentenced to six months after refusing a suggestion by the Lord Chief Justice that he should tender an apology.

This prosecution arose out of an editorial I had written on the action of Mr. Justice Rigby Swift in imposing sentences, varying from eight to eighteen months' hard labour, on three workers charged with distributing revolutionary leaflets among soldiers. I had rather let myself go in this leader and I suppose that I was somewhat under the influence of the fact that the same gentleman had sent me to prison for twelve months in 1925. The editorial, which recalled that Swift was a former Tory M.P., referred to him as a "bewigged puppet" … This, apparently, was its chief crime. Lord Chief Justice Hewart said that the words of the *Daily Worker* were a "gross and outrageous contempt of court."

I felt somewhat ashamed at the time that I was not in the dock along with my comrades, but it was then our policy not to disclose the name of the editor officially in order to provide a measure of protection for him. Our comrades acquitted themselves well in the dock. As the trial closed the precincts of the court echoed with slogans of "Hands off the *Daily Worker!*"

In the course of his speech in defence, Frank Paterson said: "Rigby Swift is a puppet of the ruling class—as are all the judges of this country. The capitalist State is the organised dictatorship of capitalism and every section of the State—parliament, the judiciary, the church and the armed forces are used in order to suppress the working class. The *Daily Worker* has spoken the truth and I stand by every word of it."

Nothing daunted by this first clash with the courts, which was to be followed by many others, our staff buckled down to its job. The expense of the action had, however, been somewhat of a strain on our limited finances, which were definitely getting into bad shape. Pencils and pads for the editorial were strictly rationed and our business manager even, so it was said, checked the level of the ink in the inkwells.

On August 25 the blow fell. The number of our pages had to be reduced from six to four. But the six-pager was retained for Saturdays and a special drive for week-end sales, which was soon to become a strikingly successful feature of *Daily Worker* activity, was introduced. By November we were selling 5,000 extra of the Saturday issue.

At that time we were not held in very high repute by our critics, especially those in the House of Lords. In November, 1930, the elderly Lord Parmoor, the father of Sir Stafford Cripps, and then Lord President of the Council in the Labour Government, said in the House of Lords: "What is this *Daily Worker*? I do not know whether it ever appeared, except on January 1, 1930, and then there were only a few hundred copies." Thereupon Lord Brentford—better known as Sir William Joynson-Hicks or "Jix"—solemnly wrote to *The Times* stating that the *Daily Worker* appeared every day and offering to supply Lord Parmoor with a copy daily. But our circulation did not go up by one copy as the aged lord stated that he could not "undertake to add the *Daily Worker* to my already overburdened task of daily reading."

A couple of months later, Lord Ponsonby dismissed us as a "twopenny-halfpenny paper produced in a London slum." And at a later date, Mr. Justice Humphreys contemptuously referred to us as this "so-called newspaper" in much the same way as Mr. Herbert Morrison described us as "only half a newspaper" when he was justifying our suppression in 1941.

Those gentlemen had, of course, standards that were entirely different from ours when it came to estimating what constituted a newspaper. And we were, in those early days, quite small and shabby in comparison to the millionaire newspapers. But we were doing a working-class job and we had not died as so many of our enemies had foretold. We therefore saw in those many contemptuous references a disguised tribute to our strength and influence. The *Daily Worker* might be despised, but it could not be ignored. We ended our first year with the feeling of satisfaction that we had survived the worst. It had been very tough going but we were firmly established and ready to face whatever the future held for us.

Apart from boycotts, financial difficulties and prosecutions we had had a very exciting time politically. The year had been dominated by the deepening economic crisis and growing unemployment which had followed in the wake of the American crash which took place in the autumn of 1929. By the end of the year the number of registered unemployed had risen to over two million. We, naturally, had given a large part of our space to the struggle of the unemployed for decent scales of benefit and relief, and many were the epic stories that we printed about these struggles and the great hunger march on London.

Our fight was strongly directed against the Labour Government which, in its efforts to get out of the crisis, was leading the rationalisation drive in industry, piling up unemployment and ferociously attacking wages. Our very first number carried as its main story on the front page a report of the strike of the

Yorkshire woollen workers against wage cuts of 2s. in the pound. The headline streamer was "Woollen Workers Take The Field; Mass Strikes Against Wage Reductions." We threw ourselves heart and soul into the Workers' Charter campaign which was waged around a series of demands representing the immediate interests of the working class.

On the international field the struggle between the imperialist powers had considerably sharpened as was shown at the London naval conference, where the two imperialist giants fought a battle for world supremacy but where they both united in their opposition to the Soviet Union and hastened their preparations for war against the land of Socialism. German Fascism made a striking advance, securing no less than six million votes in the election for the Reichstag. At the same time the Communist Party more than realised its hopes by polling 4,500,000 votes and securing 76 M.P.s. In India the revolutionary struggle flared up and troops revolted. But British imperialism fiercely counter-attacked and also let loose a deluge of propaganda in the form of the Report of the Simon Commission designed to show that only the British could rule India. But the *Daily Worker* tore the Simon Report to shreds in a series of powerful articles which found an echo in India as well as Britain.

One home event is worthy of special mention, namely, the publication in December of Sir Oswald Mosley's manifesto on how to revive British capitalism. Signatures to the manifesto included Aneurin Bevan, W.J. Brown, A.J. Cook, John McGovern and John Strachey. But the *Daily Worker* unhesitatingly denounced this mixed and peculiar crew, and in a leading article entitled "The British Hitler," poured scorn on the new movement and exposed the Fascist ideology behind the manifesto. We wrote: "Mosley dashes into this scene of indescribable chaos, bankruptcy, collapse and human suffering with a new set of catch phrases and capitalist remedies.... The Mosley manifesto is a programme of attack on the working class to be carried through by Fascist methods."

This analysis was to be proved perfectly correct and in the years ahead the *Daily Worker* was to play a vital rôle in the fight against the growth of Mosley's British Union which at one stage was heavily backed by the *Daily Mail* and Lord Rothermere.

## Chapter Two
# Persecution & Growth

THE SECOND YEAR of our existence was one of the most eventful in British history and it certainly provided plenty of excitement and shocks for the staff of the *Daily Worker;* for 1931 was a year of mounting economic crisis which culminated in the fall of the second Labour Government, the desertion of the Labour Party by its principal leaders, MacDonald, Snowden and Thomas, the heavy defeat of the Labour Party at the polls by the national coalition and the collapse of the gold standard.

One of the outstanding events of the year was the revolt of the sailors at Invergordon in protest against pay cuts. For its favourable comments on the action of the sailors the *Daily Worker* incurred the wrath of the authorities and was once again dragged into the courts. But nothing daunted, the *Daily Worker* stuck to its guns, increased its circulation, and at the time of the General Election was able to boast of an extra week-end circulation of 40,000 copies.

This was the year when Mosley left the Labour Party, formed the New Party and boastfully announced that 400 candidates would run on its behalf at the General Election. "The Mosley line," commented R. Palme Dutt, on March 7, "is the line to

Fascism and war.... Its importance is as a disorganising factor, employed by capitalism to head off and divert the growing discontent in the Labour Party and in all strata of the population." One of the bourgeois young bloods who followed Mosley was John Strachey, the present Food Minister. A year later Strachey wrote an article for the *Daily Worker* renouncing his fascist associations, he became a Communist sympathiser and from 1935-39 was a regular contributor to the *Daily Worker*. But having sown his wild oats he is now a dutiful member of the Labour Party.

The *Daily Worker* pressed on its fight against the growing unemployment and for the demands of the unemployed who were now coming under fire of the Labour Government. In June, when the number of registered unemployed had passed the two-and-a-half million mark, the Royal Commission on Unemployment presented its report in favour of reduced benefit for a shortened period and the payment of higher contributions.

The Report met with a tremendous wave of protest, but it was really only one part of the economy drive of the Government against the living standards of the people. At the end of July came the Report of the May Economy Committee with its proposals to save £66,500,000 on unemployment insurance, £13,850,000 on education, £3,875,000 on pay and pensions and £1,000,000 on health insurance. The total of the economies was £96,500,000, of which only £900,000 was on defence. "This brutal and ruthless attack," said the *Daily Worker,* "is made on the poorest of the poor in order to safeguard the £110 million armament bill and the £360 million yearly interest and sinking fund on the War Debt." A few days later we announced that unemployment had risen to 2,713,350, the highest figure ever known.

The Economy Report decided the fate of the Government. The Cabinet was thrown into confusion and the leadership of the country was in fact handed over to the Tories. A number of Labour Ministers, afraid of their own handiwork, hesitated, drew back and finally expressed their opposition to the cut in unemployment benefit by 10 per cent. But the most prominent held to their course, and after a number of conferences with the Tory and Liberal leaders announced their intention to form a National Government.

On August 24 the Labour Government resigned and Ramsay MacDonald, along with Thomas, Snowden and Lord Sankey formed a Coalition Government together with Baldwin for the Tories and Sir Herbert Samuel for the Liberals. The great betrayal had taken place. The Labour Party had first capitulated and then split in the face of the pressure of the big capitalists and banks. But the split produced no real change in the policy of the official Labour Party which, having first toyed with the economy proposals, resolutely avoided any call for mass action against the traitors, who together with the Tories and Liberals, were now putting their policy into action, including the hated means test. The split was, in fact, a method of bolstering up capitalist rule. On the one hand, the treachery of MacDonald had enabled the ruling class to form a strengthened Government for their own purposes while, on the other hand, the

Labour Party was enabled to appear as the opposition and as if it had no responsibility for the policies now being pursued. "MacDonald as a statesman saves the State," cynically wrote the Social-Democratic *Arbeiter-Zeitung* of Vienna, "while Henderson as the secretary of the party, saves the party."

In the weeks following the formation of the National Government there was great uproar in the country against the threatening cuts which reached its highest point with the mutiny of the Fleet at Invergordon in September against the reduced rates of naval pay. A few days later the gold standard collapsed. For the *Daily Worker* the Invergordon mutiny was a signal event which again led to police action against the paper, but this time of a more far-reaching character. On September 17, we announced the mutiny under the headline of "Sailors Join the No Cuts Fight," and the following day we published the manifesto of the sailors which declared that "we are resolved to remain as one unit refusing to sail under the new rates of pay." The day after we supported the stand made by the sailors and then the police acted.

The first intimation to our readers of what the police had got up to was the appearance of a large blank space on our front page of September 25 in which were inscribed the words "Censored by Printer." Underneath it was stated: "This space was occupied by a report dealing with the visit of detectives to the office of the *Daily Worker* yesterday." Many issues were to appear with these white spaces as our printer, Mr. W.T. Wilkinson, managing director of the Utopia Press, Ltd., had a pretty severe attack of cold feet and point blank refused to permit us to publish any items which he considered likely to get him into trouble with the authorities. Actually, old Mr. W. was arrested the same day, on a charge under the Incitement to Mutiny Act of 1797, simultaneous with the raiding of the *Daily Worker* and the confiscation of our files and documents by the Special Branch of Scotland Yard. Naturally, our issue of September 26 also contained "Censored by Printer" notices. But it also contained a call to the workers to defend their paper, an appeal for more circulation and another £500 in the Fighting Fund.

When Mr. Wilkinson appeared before the Bow Street magistrate he was granted bail on the specific condition that no matter was to appear in the *Daily Worker* "in any way touching or concerning the armed forces of His Majesty." The official censorship was thus at work.

At the time of the raid the police also introduced a censorship on their own account. I was informed by the detective-inspector in charge of the raid that all material for the paper would have to pass through the hands of his men, who, he said, "will pass anything that is not inflammatory." At the press, police officers examined page proofs, struck out a reader's letter, changed the headline on the report of a speech by Tom Mann and also deleted paragraphs from the report. It was also admitted by the police that they had no warrant for the searching of the editorial offices of the *Daily Worker,* but they went right ahead and ransacked every cupboard and table and then carried off their spoil in two vans. Our issue of September 26 carried a blank space marked "Censored by Police." Questioned in the House of Commons the following week on these incidents, the Hon. Oliver Stanley, Under-Secretary for the Home Office, point blank denied that any police censorship had been applied!

One amusing result of Mr. Wilkinson's strict adherence to his bail terms was an announcement in one of our blank spaces that it was to have been occupied by a report from a Santiago correspondent on a revolt in the Chilean Navy. Mr. Wilkinson was taking no risks. But it did not save him. On October 21 he was sentenced at the Old Bailey to nine months in the second division. For the prosecution, Sir Percival Clarke, addressing the jury, said: "This is no political case, you must put political views out of your minds." Clarke also denied that the police had censored the *Daily Worker* and the judge blandly observed: "It is the first time I have heard of anyone censoring the Press. The Press are as free to express opinions as anybody else." He then sent Mr. Wilkinson to prison.

It was equally the intention of the police to arrest the nominal proprietors of the *Daily Worker* as they had the previous year in the Rigby Swift case but they were not able to lay hands on them immediately. Frank Paterson was not arrested until the end of October and Frank Priestley remained at large until the end of December. Both these comrades had already served a term of imprisonment on behalf of the paper, but they again firmly stood their ground.

Frank Paterson was sentenced to two years' imprisonment and Priestley to three years' penal servitude. Both of them made fearless and inspiring speeches from the dock. The charges against them, preferred under the Incitement to Mutiny Act of 1797, were of endeavouring to seduce persons in H.M. Forces from their duty and allegiance to His Majesty and to incite and stir up such persons to acts of mutiny.

The authorities apparently hoped to finish the paper entirely by frightening off the printer. "What!" exclaimed a prominent detective after the Wilkinson trial, "is that damned paper still coming out?" On the contrary, our position was strengthened and the workers rallied to our cause. On the night of the police raid two thousand workers had marched in solidarity to our office from East London. And friends of the paper had provided the relatively modest sum needed to buy out Mr. Wilkinson and secure a controlling interest in the Utopia Press.

Another Invergordon mutiny trial which was staged at this period was of considerable interest to the *Daily Worker* as it involved a young sub-editor on our staff, W.G. Shepherd, as well as George Allison, who was then secretary of the National Minority Movement. Both were charged with attempting to distribute subversive leaflets to sailors. The principal witness for the prosecution was a sailor who was acting under the instructions of his officer. Both made a fighting political stand in the court and were then heavily sentenced, Allison to three years' penal servitude and Shepherd to 20 months' hard labour. Bill Shepherd rejoined us after his release and has been with us ever since with the exception of his period of military service. He came to me in 1930 straight from a building site—he is a woodworker by trade. He is now a chief sub-editor, and all through these years has proved himself to be a loyal and talented worker for our cause.

During this period of the trials we were constantly beset by detectives, and members of the Special Branch were on our doorstep peering at every person who passed in and out.

The General Election in October resulted in an overwhelming victory for the National Government and Labour representation was heavily reduced. All of the 26 Communist candidates were defeated but they put up a great fight and the *Daily Worker,* which went up to six pages daily for the election campaign, made a brave show every day with its cogent arguments around the slogans—Not a Penny Off the Dole, Not a Penny Off Wages, Down with the National Starvation Government.

The circulation of the paper was now on the rise, especially at week-ends: we began 1932 with a feeling of elation and big anniversary meetings were held up and down the country. After two years of publication and the successful survival of two big prosecutions, there was a general feeling that the paper had now come to stay. Our critics still gave vent to their venom but they no longer foretold our early demise. They fell back on the hoary lie that we were kept going by Moscow gold.

We ourselves sometimes wished that we had supplies of that elusive gold when we anxiously surveyed our financial problems and wondered how to get a few pounds more. During our first two years the Fighting Fund had raised £9,000, but as we were practically without advertisement revenue this sum was by no means enough. Sometimes we had to cut down to four pages. Photographs were rare. Economy was always the cry.

By March of 1932 we had raised our first £10,000 and from then onwards our Fighting Fund was set at £350 a month. In 1948, sixteen years later, we set ourselves the aim of raising ten times that amount every month! It is the measure of our progress and of the place that the *Daily Worker* has won in the hearts of the working people. In those old days we were always announcing a new grave crisis and calling for a renewed effort in terms of donations and circulation drives. The wolf was always at the door, but somehow or the other we just managed to keep him at bay.

In the opening months of that year the *Daily Worker* took up the fight against the Japanese warmongers who had launched their war against China with the terrible bombardment of Shanghai. We warned of the world consequences of this horrible deed—a warning that in later years was to come only too true—and carried on a persistent campaign for the stopping of the transport of munitions to Japan.

By March we were publishing cables from Walter Holmes, our special correspondent in Shanghai, in which he gave a vivid description of the horrors committed by the Japanese and outlined their imperialist aims. Holmes had previously been reporting for us in Moscow and had transferred his activities to Shanghai shortly after the outbreak of the Japanese war. In latter years he did another remarkably effective job for the *Daily Worker* as our war correspondent in Abyssinia and he also covered the

Nuremberg trial. Holmes is an all-round newspaperman, cool headed, of wide experience and ready to turn his hand to any job on the paper.

We had cherished certain hopes of getting through this year without more court cases but by August we were involved with Mr W.H. Hutchinson, the ex-president of the Amalgamated Engineering Union, who charged us with contempt of court for some remarks we had made regarding his dismissal from his post on the grounds of drunkenness. But we were merely fined £50, our printers £25 and Mr. Hutchinson had to pay his own costs.

Much more grave for us was the trial of our manager, Clarence Mason, at Castleford in November on a charge of publishing a defamatory libel on the West Riding police. This charge arose out of a report in the *Daily Worker* that a worker who died following a police charge against an unemployed demonstration had not died from natural causes, as stated at the inquest, but as a result of his brutal batoning by the police. Mason was subsequently sent to prison for six months in the second division and our printers, the Utopia Press, were fined £500.

Shortly before this affair Mason had also been fined £500 for the publication of a resolution protesting against the arrest of Sid Elias, one of the leaders of the National Unemployed Workers' Movement. Elias was subsequently sentenced to two years' imprisonment. The resolution, which described the case against Elias as a "frame-up," was held by the Lord Chief Justice to be a gross contempt of court. Our printers were also involved in this charge and fines totalling £550 were imposed on them. The total fines in the two cases amounted therefore to £1,550. The new managing director of the Utopia Press was our comrade Kay Beauchamp. Not being in a position to pay her fine, Kay was detained in Holloway Prison at His Majesty's pleasure and released only after five months in its none too pleasant confines.

These experiences served as a salutary reminder to us that our columns were being closely watched by the authorities and that great care would have to be exercised by our editorial staff in order not to give our enemies a chance. Emphasis was therefore laid on the legal examination of every item of news before publication and this system is still strongly maintained. It has not saved us, however, from a number of libel actions, most of which were undertaken from a political motive.

In any case, 1932 was marked by an extremely hostile attitude to Communist activities on the part of the authorities and many of our comrades were thrown into prison on various pretexts. In February, Arthur Horner and 28 of his comrades were sent to prison on a charge of "unlawful assembly and inciting to riot," arising from their actions in preventing the eviction of a worker from his home in Mardy for rate arrears. Horner got the heaviest sentence—fifteen months' hard labour. In November, Wal Hannington got three months for a speech likely to cause disaffection among the London police, and in December came the strangest case of all, the arrest of Tom Mann, then 76, under an act of Edward III as a possible disturber of the peace. This action was taken because of Tom Mann's connection with the National Unemployed Workers' Movement, which was then organising monster demonstrations in London and throughout the country.

In binding over Tom Mann, the magistrate, Sir Charles Biron, made the following amazing statement: "There is no criminal charge and no question of imprisonment. The proceedings were merely to enforce a law which had been the law of the land from time immemorial for the protection of public order. It was merely a preventive measure." But Tom Mann stood his ground, refused to give any guarantees about an offence he had not committed, and was thereupon sentenced to two months' imprisonment. Commented the *Daily Worker:* "Could there be a more glaring confirmation of the correctness of the Communist Party's contention that the working class is being ruled by a capitalist dictatorship in this country against which the workers must fight with all their strength?"

An extraordinary feature of many of these trials was the manner in which the police and learned judges showed how strongly they were under the influence of the anti-Soviet propaganda then being conducted by the Press and the Government. Mr. Justice Charles was so blind to the cause of working-class dissatisfaction in Britain that when sentencing Sid Elias to two years' imprisonment he declared: "It is only because the British working class is so inherently law-abiding that only one or two in a thousand are influenced by the advice that you give them at the behest and direction of your friends in Moscow."

But the palm for stupidity must surely be handed to the police-inspector in the Horner case who solemnly stated in court: "Horner pays frequent visits to Russia and the source of his income is not known. It is only presumed that he is well paid by Russia for his efforts to destroy the peace of this country. During his absence things are normal at Mardy, which prior to his advent was a prosperous mining district."

During these hard years the *Daily Worker* had steadfastly maintained a fighting political line and had correctly analysed home and international events. It had been the first newspaper to signalise the Japanese attack on China and seizure of Manchuria as events which would hasten the outbreak of a new world war. The *Daily Worker* had explained that capitalism in the throes of its terrible crisis was giving birth to Fascism and it warned that the German ruling class was preparing to bring Hitler to power in order to destroy those rights and liberties which the German masses were utilising in pursuance of their struggles. It welcomed the decline of the Hitler forces and the gains of the Communists in the election of November, 1932, but warned that precisely because of this setback there was the danger that the Fascists would be hurriedly pushed to power.

Alone among the Press, the *Daily Worker* told the truth about the great Socialist successes and peace policy of the Soviet Union. Vivid, inspiring articles about the Soviet Union filled its columns in contrast to the filth and trash in the rest of the Press.

At home, the National Government and the employers continued their attacks on the living standards of the employed and unemployed, took the first steps in the rearmament policy and began to look with great favour on the rise of the Nazis. A strong and reactionary Germany already occupied a definite place in their scheme of the future which included war against the Soviet Union. But the ruling class was also depressed and uncertain. They were afraid of what the ensuing years held for them. Their views were summed up in the British Note to the U.S. on the question of war debts: "Signs of the paralysis of trade and the threat of bankruptcy and of financial collapse … The international monetary mechanism without which the modern world cannot effectively conduct its daily life is being broken to pieces with all the manifold forms of privation and distress which this involves."

The following year was to witness the desperate attempt of capitalism to save itself by the bringing of Fascism to power in Germany. It was answered by a great extension of the united front of the working class and extension of the activities of the Communist Parties and their Press. In this fight the *Daily Worker* played a worthy part and greatly increased its influence and prestige.

After nearly three years of strenuous participation in the production of the paper I left the editorial chair* towards the

---

* Because of the threat of prosecution continually hanging over the *Daily Worker*, no successor to Rust was publicly named, but the paper was edited by Jimmy Shields, Idris Cox, R. Palme Dutt, Dave Springhall and J.R. Campbell before Rust returned to the hotseat in 1939.—J.E.

end of 1932 in order to act as representative of the British Communist Party to the Executive Committee of the Communist International in Moscow. I did not return to the editorship until seven years later, soon after the outbreak of the war in 1939. But I kept a close connection with the *Daily Worker* during my period abroad and also when I was Communist Party organiser in Lancashire and national organiser at the Party Centre. From December, 1937, to July, 1938, I was the paper's war correspondent in Spain and derived great inspiration from my close association with the British Battalion of the immortal International Brigade.

## Chapter Three
# The People's Front against Fascism

THE YEAR 1933 was dominated by that event of its opening months, the coming to power of Hitler in Germany, which was preceded by the burning of the Reichstag by the Nazis on February 27 in order to pull off the greatest anti-Communist stunt in history on the eve of the General Election. In March, Hitler was appointed Chancellor by President Hindenburg. The Nazis now had the State within their grasp and there thus began the unfolding of those dark events which through intrigue, murder and suppression were to lead up to the unleashing of the world war and the final crushing of the Nazi gang.

The triumph of Fascism in Germany signified the imposition of a bloody tyranny on the German people. But this advance of Fascism, as Stalin pointed out, was not only a proof of the weakness of the working class and the result of betrayal by the Social Democratic Party, but also a symptom of the weakness of the ruling class who were no longer able to rule by the old democratic methods. The *Daily Worker* clearly grasped this point and threw itself into the fight against Fascism with the confidence that it could be overthrown by the united front of the people.

These events did in fact result in a widespread development of the united front, the development of co-operation between the Communist and Socialist parties and the formation of the People's Front in France and Spain. On March 8, the *Daily Worker* published the manifesto of the Communist International calling on the Communist Parties to approach the Socialist Parties with programmes of common action against Fascism and attacks on living standards. It recommended that no criticisms should be directed against Socialist organisations during the period of common action.

This call, which brought about a sharp turn in the relations between the Communist and Socialist workers, was debated with great sincerity and vigour in the Presidium of the Communist International. I took part in that debate on behalf of the British Party and I know that we all felt that we were speaking under the shadow of great historical events. Shortly after I was sent to Berlin in order to make contact with Wilhelm Pieck.* By that time the Communist Party was illegal and the Nazi terror had begun but the comrades were still taking great risks and Pieck was moving about fairly openly with only a beard as a disguise. After a visit to other countries I made my way back to Moscow and stopped again in Berlin where, to my horror, I read in the newspapers of the arrest of George Dimitrov on a charge of

......................................................

* Then a leading member of the Communist Party of Germany, Pieck would later become the first president of the German Democratic Republic.—J.E.

complicity in the burning down of the Reichstag.

Three days after the publication of the manifesto of the Communist International the *Daily Worker* featured on its front page the letter of the Communist Party to the Labour Party making proposals for united front action. This letter was, of course, rejected, but it sowed a seed and the widespread united front activities which developed during the following years can undoubtedly be attributed to this Communist initiative.

For the *Daily Worker* the year opened up with a financial crisis. Nothing unusual in that the reader will say. But this time we were really in severe difficulties and Harry Pollitt, who has always been unfailing in his devotion to the paper, had to step in with an appeal for a loan of £2,000 from readers. At that time we were again down to four pages daily. The response to Pollitt's appeal was so good that we got the six pages back in March. But in July we had to come out with another appeal on behalf of the Fighting Fund which had been lagging somewhat. We had, however, raised over £12,000 for this Fund during the first three years of our existence, so we did not have very much to grumble about.

It should be remembered that in those years our four and six pages looked puny compared to the twenty and twenty-four page capitalist giants which not only offered the reader much more, at least in quantity, for his money but free gifts as well. The free gift war was raging pretty fiercely in 1933, and in September we reported a proposal of the *Express* newspapers to set aside another £100,000 as sinews of war.

In November, a libel action taken against us by Ernest Bevin came before the King's Bench Division and Mr. Justice Horridge assessed the damage done to that gentleman at the not inconsiderable sum of £7,000, plus costs. The value of Labour leaders has gone up, remarked Harry Pollitt, when he compared Bevin's £7,000 with the £2,000 awarded to J.H. Thomas in his libel action against the Communists in 1921. Whether Mr. Justice Horridge really thought that Bevin was worth £7,000 or whether he thought that this sum was just about sufficient to ruin the *Daily Worker,* I do not know. Sufficient to say that we could not afford to pay and therefore did not pay.

Bevin based his libel claim on an article in the *Daily Worker* of September 29, 1932, which accused him of being "an agent of the London General Omnibus Company," a "wage-cutting ally of Lord Ashfield," and of "lying and trickery." Proceedings were instituted against the Utopia Press, Ltd., and Clarence Mason, former proprietor of the *Daily Worker.* Mason conducted his own defence and stood his ground very well despite intervention by the judge. The article complained of dealt with the question of bus wages and conditions in London and the negotiations for which Bevin was responsible.

When the *Daily Worker* was initially approached by Bevin's solicitors regarding this article, an offer was made to give prominence, equal to that given to the article, to Bevin's views on the issues and also to correct any misstatements of fact. Most trade unionists will agree that this was a fair offer and, in fact, the only way of settling a conflict of view within the Labour movement. But Bevin would have none of it. He insisted on court proceedings and engaged as counsel none other than that political chameleon, Sir William Jowitt, who later became the Lord Chancellor in the third Labour Government.

Certain of Sir William's remarks are worth recalling here as a revelation of his attitude, if not that of Bevin's, to the rank and file trade unionist. He stated that the defendants should have admitted their error and have apologised for the article. That would have been the English course. He continued:

"They won't. Why? Do you think that it is partly because they realise they have nothing to lose? Or is it—as vile a thing as one can come across—that they think they can get control of the working class by spreading lies and slanders, by deluding not very highly educated, rather ignorant men, discrediting their leaders? There's something thoroughly un-English about that. I'm not going to say where it comes from."

To this farrago of nonsense, Clarence Mason returned the dignified plea that the facts in the alleged libel were true, and that the expressions of opinion were fair comment on a matter of public interest. One of the witnesses he called was Bert Papworth, the well known bus conductor who is now a very active member of the Editorial Board of the *Daily Worker,* and whose evidence was given in characteristic style which evoked the immediate displeasure of the judge. Describing what happened at a busmen's delegate conference, Papworth said: "After twenty minutes' pandemonium—" Judge: "I don't want to hear

about that." Asked by Mason what happened at a later conference, Papworth answered: "This was one of the biggest fiddles
ever perpetrated on London busmen." Judge: "I cannot allow
that." Nevertheless, "Pappie" succeeded in getting his points
over in court.

Eight years later the *Daily Worker* was again to run foul of Sir
William Jowitt when he appeared on behalf of certain members
of the General Council of the Trades Union Congress who
considered that we had libelled them (p.158 below).

Clarence Mason later announced that the damages awarded
by Mr. Justice Horridge were his personal responsibility, together
with the printers, and not the responsibility of the then owners
of the *Daily Worker*. "None of the money raised by the Fighting
Fund," he added, "or by sales of the paper will go towards
these damages." Final comment on the Bevin libel action was
the report in our issue of December 9 that the Busmen's Rank
and File Movement had won a majority on the Central Bus
Committee by democratic election. In an editorial that day we
argued for Bevin's benefit that the *Daily Worker* had spoken for
that majority.

Since the formation of the National Government in the
previous year relations with the Soviet Union had been systematically worsening and after the coming of Hitler to power in
March, Press lords and politicians began to display a marked
regard for the Nazis. "Hitler," wrote Lord Rothermere in the
*Daily Mail* on July 10, "has converted a despondent and embit-
tered nation into one radiant with hope and enthusiasm." Even

the *Daily Herald* set out to prove that the Nazis were really not quite as bad as they had been painted. In a leading article entitled "Hitler's May Day," it wrote:

"The 'National Socialists'—it is essential to remember— call themselves 'Socialist' as well as 'National.' Their 'Socialism' is not the Socialism of the Labour Party, or that of any recognised Socialist Party in other countries. But in many ways it is a creed that is anathema to the big landlords, the big industrialists, and the big financiers. And the Nazi leaders are bound to go forward with the 'Socialist' side of their programme."

The comment of the *Daily Worker* on this Labourite flirtation with Fascism was sharp and to the point:

"Put into plain language, what we have here is a deliberate friendly handshake extended to German Fascism, which is lyingly depicted as being opposed sharply to the interests of the capitalist class in Germany, and out for the establishment of Socialism ... It also expresses a swinging into line on their part with British imperialism in its attitude of striving to utilise the support of Hitler for anti-Soviet intervention purposes."

It was in this atmosphere of developing friendship towards Fascism and of increasing hostility towards the Soviet Union that the National Government found itself confronted with the trial in Moscow of the Metropolitan Vickers' engineers, who were charged with sabotage and espionage. Two of these engineers, Thornton and Macdonald, were sentenced to three and two years' imprisonment respectively. The Government not only stood by its spies, it also declared war on Anglo-Soviet trade and prohibited the import from Russia of such vital commodities as petroleum, butter, raw cotton, timber and grain. Public Prosecutor at the trial was A.Y. Vyshinsky, who many years later was to build himself a big world reputation as Soviet spokesman in the United Nations.

I happened to be in Moscow at the time and attended all the sessions of the trial which provided me with a concentrated and instructive lesson on international affairs. The reports published in the British Press were utterly fantastic and we had hearty laughs over the *Daily Mail* story that the prisoners were given "Thibetan drugs" in order to make them confess. It was well known in Moscow that these spies had freely confessed to their crimes because they did not expect that the British Government would stand by them. Later it was made clear to them that if they would repudiate their statements and stand firm on pleas of innocence they would in return get full official protection.

The trial was very ably reported for the *Daily Worker* by our special correspondent in Moscow, Reg Bishop, whose untimely death took place in 1948. Known familiarly to everyone as "Bish," he was a mountain of a man and a hive of energy. I always regarded "Bish" as a born journalist because of the way he combined an ability for easy writing with dash and go and a brimming versatility. He was also superb on the public platform and achieved a big reputation as an expert on the Soviet Union. In our early days he had contributed satirical articles signed

**Joy-Day in the Royal Rabbit-warren**

This Maro cartoon of November 29, 1934 earned the cartoonist an extra guinea when the Duchess of Atholl reproduced it without permission

"Trundley" and later on covered the music hall for us.

Another talented comrade who came to us early in 1933 was W.C. Rowney[*] ("Maro"), our cartoonist, who died a hero's death as a member of the International Brigade in Spain. He fell at Jarama in February, 1937. Old readers of the *Daily Worker* will remember him very well, especially his delightful "Royal Rabbit-Warren" cartoon on the marriage of the Duke of Kent to the Greek Princess Marina in December, 1934[†]. Maro subsequently touched the Duchess of Atholl for a guinea for this cartoon! It appears that her Grace, who ran an anti-Soviet outfit

..............................................

[*] Actually W.D. (William Desmond).—J.E.

[†] Actually November 29—J.E.

called the Christian Protest Movement, was so enraged with the cartoon that she had it reproduced full size in her official organ in order to arouse the indignation of the faithful, whereupon Maro pointed out that his copyright had been infringed and demanded £2 2s. as reproduction fee. But they fobbed him off with a mere guinea.

Under the influence of the increasing desire for unity against Fascism, the Independent Labour Party had decided at its Derby conference to approach the Communist International "with a view to ascertaining in what way the I.L.P. may assist in the work of the International." Various limited united front activities had taken place between the I.L.P. and the Communist Party, but the influence of the Right-Wing leaders of the Brockway* type prevented a firm agreement being reached. An exchange of letters took place between the Communist International and the I.L.P. and there was a good deal of discussion in the columns of the *Daily Worker* arising from the suggestion of the Communist International that the I.L.P. should affiliate as a sympathising organisation. But nothing concrete emerged and the I.L.P. continued to drift on to decline, trying to face both ways and as a result losing its influence with all sections of the Labour movement so that today it is a mere sect.

The concluding months of 1933 witnessed the gathering force of the world movement exposing the Nazi responsibility for the

........................................

* Fenner Brockway, then chairman of the Independent Labour Party.—J.E.

burning of the Reichstag and for the release of the giant-hearted
Dimitrov whose trial began at Leipzig on September 22. A week
before the Leipzig trial opened there began in London a "Legal
Commission of Inquiry Into the Burning of the Reichstag."
Opener was Sir Stafford Cripps, K.C., M.P., and among the
famous lawyers constituting the tribunal were its chairman, Mr.
D.N. Pritt, K.C., Dr. Branting, of Sweden, and Signor Nitti,
of Italy. Day by day the *Daily Worker* devoted great prominence to these proceedings, which were covered by its special
correspondent, R. Page Arnot. The Commission reached the
conclusion that none of the accused Communists caused the
fire or were in any way connected with it.

Dimitrov's noble and inspiring demeanour at Leipzig was fully
reported in the *Daily Worker*. "I am a Communist, it is true. I
am a proletarian revolutionary," he declared to the court on the
third day. Not for one moment did he flinch. Three times he was
expelled from the court, but he returned on November 4 to turn
the tables on Goering, who in impotent rage shrieked: "Take
that crook out of here." Dimitrov was expelled for the fourth
time and as he left the court he heard another frenzied cry from
Goering: "Wait until we get you in our hands." But Dimitrov
was rescued from the hands of the Nazis, rescued by the international protest movement in which the *Daily Worker* played an
honourable part. The court was compelled to acquit Dimitrov
and, although he was still held in prison, he was subsequently
released on the representations of the Soviet Government and
arrived in Moscow on February 27, 1934. Dimitrov subsequently

became the secretary of the Communist International and I had the pleasure of greeting him when I visited the Soviet Union in November, 1938, as a member of a trade union delegation. Later he became the Prime Minister of the People's Republic of Bulgaria—the true Father of his country.

Another great trial in connection with which the *Daily Worker* helped to organise the protest movement from the very first day of its publication was the trial at Meerut, India, of the 27 leaders of Indian trade unionism, among them three Britishers. This was a trial of most extraordinary length. The arrests, on a charge of "conspiracy against the King-Emperor," took place in March, 1929, the trial began in the summer of that year and lasted for three years. Sentence was not pronounced until January, 1933, when heavy terms of imprisonment and transportation were imposed. In August, 1933, several of the prisoners were acquitted on appeal and other sentences heavily reduced.

Among the prisoners were Ben Bradley, noted London engineer, who is now the circulation manager of the *Daily Worker,* and Lester Hutchinson, who went to India as a journalist and edited the paper of the Workers' and Peasants' Party. In 1945, Hutchinson was elected to Parliament as Labour Member for Rusholme, Manchester, and has distinguished himself by his consistent left-wing stand in the House of Commons. He has contributed a number of articles to the *Daily Worker.*

During the following two years a number of technical improvements were effected in the *Daily Worker*—on January 1, 1934, we had our first modern type dress, designed by Allen

Hutt—and the paper became more popular. We also received notice to quit from our Tabernacle Street landlords with the result that we shifted a few hundred yards to Cayton Street, off the City Road. Here we again acquired an old warehouse, but it was much roomier and we were able to bring our editorial and printing offices under one roof. The notice to quit—it applied both to Tabernacle Street and to the Utopia Press in Worship Street—came soon after the Bevin libel action and our enemies thought it was to be really the fatal blow. But after months of effort we finally obtained the new premises and also acquired another rotary machine. This latter was absolutely essential as, otherwise, we would have had to stop printing during the process of removal and assembly of the machinery.

The news about our notice to quit was not broken to our readers until all our plans had been completed. Then came the announcement on September 29, 1934, with an appeal by Harry Pollitt for £2,500 to carry through the job. "The blunt truth about the present situation is that we are fighting for our very existence," wrote Pollitt. The result of the appeal was splendid. By November 1, £2,551 had come in of which £1,124 was in donations.

The transference was a trying job but finally everything was installed in the paper's new home at Cayton Street and the first issue off the new rotary appeared on January 14, 1935. It was a great achievement and the staff were proud of their new offices which had been made shipshape with the aid of voluntary work from a number of sympathetic craftsmen. The main drive was now switched to circulation with the emphasis that the dou-bling of the circulation was the main way to the solution of our financial problems. That, however, was easier said than done as the wholesalers' boycott was still operative and the getting of the paper to the newsagent fell chiefly on our own distributive apparatus. Moreover, we had no free gifts to offer. New readers had to be won on the basis of political conviction. But the cam-paign was pushed ahead and good results obtained. The readers and the members of the Communist Party felt themselves very close to the paper for they knew that its life literally depended on their efforts.

During this period we were singularly free from libel actions of any importance and the police were inclined to let us alone. Finally, they even stopped hanging around our doorstep and in March, 1935, we triumphantly announced that the Special Branch detectives were no longer to be seen in the vicinity of Cayton Street.

There can be no question at all that the *Daily Worker* greatly improved during 1934-35 both in appearance and in its trenchant handling of current events. It was becoming a political force and its views were widely noted. In April, 1935, it announced a 50 per cent. increase in circulation compared to the previous September and promised an eight-page paper in the following October if the campaign was kept up. On October 1, the eight-page *Daily Worker* duly appeared. Communist Party membership was also on the increase.

Both the Communist Party and the *Daily Worker* were now

beginning to reap the fruits of their persistent fight against the economic crisis and in defence of the living standards of the people, of their resolute opposition to Fascism and warnings regarding the gravity of the war danger, of their proud reporting of the Socialist successes of the Soviet Union and explanation of its peace policy. The call made by the 7th Congress of the Communist International in the summer of 1935 for the formation of a People's Front further helped to show people where the Communists stood. In November of that year the Communist Party decided to apply for affiliation to the Labour Party.

During these two years the people were beginning to awaken. Anger was growing against the home policy of the National Government and grave concern was being expressed about the deterioration of the international situation. At home there were various strikes and unemployed hunger marches continued, although some improvement in the economic situation was taking place. The *Daily Worker* was the only newspaper which regularly featured these marches, but they did not meet with the approval of the trade union bureaucracy which was becoming increasingly anti-Communist. In June, 1935, Mr. Walter Citrine, secretary of the Trades Union Congress, was made a Knight Commander of the Most Excellent Order of the British Empire for services rendered. The conferring of this title provoked widespread protest in the Labour movement. Commented the *Daily Worker:* "That Citrine is singled out for British capitalism's mark of appreciation is not surprising. He stands out as one of the most virulent opponents of working-class unity ...

Those whom capitalism hates and fears don't figure in a King's Honours List."

It was in those years likewise that the peace desires of the people began to take more definite shape consequent upon the rise of Fascism and entry of the Soviet Union into the League of Nations in September, 1934, where it promptly put forward its famous disarmament proposals. Mussolini's attack on Abyssinia and the despicable sell-out arranged between Hoare and Laval* aroused the conscience of millions and made them realise the dangers they were facing.

The *Daily Worker* dealt prominently with the war in Abyssinia and explained the meaning of British policy in refusing to apply effective sanctions. The refusal to close the Suez Canal and to stop petrol supplies to Italy was characterised as part of the appeasement policy towards Fascism. From the battlefields, where the Blackshirts had resorted to the use of poison gas, Walter Holmes sent a series of vivid dispatches and photographs. Incidentally, he also represented *The Times* as well as the *Daily Worker* during part of his time there.

The appeasement of the German Nazis in order to strengthen the Hitlerite State for war against the Soviet Union began clearly to emerge with the tolerance of the introduction of conscription

........................................

* The attempt by Britain's Foreign Secretary Samuel Hoare and the French Prime Minister Pierre Laval to hand Mussolini large chunks of Abyssinia in exchange for a truce. When the pact came to light the uproar forced both Hoare and Laval to resign.—J.E.

by Hitler in March, 1935, and the signing of the Anglo-German Naval Agreement three months later. The comment in the *Daily Worker* struck a note of alarm. About conscription in Germany it wrote: "This latest step on Hitler's part is the direct outcome of the policy conducted and pursued by the National Government. All along the National Government has assisted and encouraged the war plans of Nazi Germany. It deliberately approved of Germany's secret rearmament and supported legalising it in order to further the most deadly aims against the Soviet Union." It was equally outspoken on the Naval Agreement: "The Naval Pact agreed upon between Britain and Germany is a war pact. It is a deliberate blow directed against the forces striving for peace. It is a step which provides, not for the limitation of naval armaments, but for their expansion with a view to war."

Despite this pro-Fascist policy, Stanley Baldwin, who that June had become Premier in place of Ramsay MacDonald, still posed as a man of peace and set out to win the General Election on the basis of that pose, thus conciliating the millions who had taken part in the Peace Ballot* earlier in the year. "I give you my word that there will be no great armaments," he said, and then afterwards openly admitted that this was a deliberate and cruel deception of the electorate.

...................................................

* A national ballot organised by the League of Nations Union in which 11 million voters overwhelmingly backed arms reduction, League of Nations membership, collective security and a ban on selling arms for private profit.—J.E.

The *Daily Worker* plunged itself into the General Election campaign with great gusto and called for support of the Labour candidates. In the interests of unity the Communist Party had decided to withdraw all of its candidates except Harry Pollitt and William Gallacher. The latter was returned for West Fife as the first Member of Parliament directly elected as a Communist. Labour was recovering from the debacle of 1931, but it obtained only 154 seats compared to the 431 obtained by the Tories and their "National" stooges.

The two Royal events, the marriage of the Duke of Kent to a Greek princess and the King's Silver Jubilee, which occurred during this period, gave the *Daily Worker* an opportunity to enter the lists against the pomp and extravagance of the Monarchy. There was certainly punch in these headlines on the marriage:

## OUT OF WORK PRINCESS SIGNS ON FOR DOLE
## £500 A WEEK DEAL TODAY
## YOU PAY FOR HER WEDDING BELLS

In an editorial on the Jubilee the *Daily Worker* said:

"Today the slobber of imperialist propaganda reaches its zenith. The gilt and glitter of the royal cavalcade passes by. Tomorrow there will still be the means test, 2,000,000 unemployed, Gresford miners on strike, speed-up in the factories, working-class mothers and babies dying for want of nourishment, bloody repression in the subject Colonial countries. Ladies and gentlemen of imperialism, have your day today, raise your glasses in your 'Loyal Toasts.'

Tomorrow we workers will have ours, and when we strike we will strike hard and end for ever your rule and your luxury."

Prominent among our staff in those days was Claud Cockburn, known to our readers by his pen name, Frank Pitcairn. He joined us in the early months of 1935 after resigning from his post in the Washington office of *The Times* in spite of the supplications of his editor, Geoffrey Dawson, who wrote an urgent personal letter in order to persuade Cockburn to remain on.

Cockburn was an extremely gifted writer with an abnormally sharp political mind. The combination of these two qualities, plus personal charm and a flair as a raconteur, made him into the best diplomatic correspondent of the day. I have always felt sorry for *The Times* that they lost him. Cockburn specialised on foreign affairs, but like all first-class journalists, he could turn his hand to any story. We used him on home affairs as well as foreign and he was often available as a re-write man when a story needed to be polished up and made to sparkle.

## Chapter Four
# We Fought for Spain and Unity

THE STORY OF the *Daily Worker's* fight for Republican Spain against the Fascist attack launched by Hitler and Mussolini through their agent Franco in July, 1936, is the greatest in its entire history. For over two years the *Daily Worker* upheld the cause of Spanish democracy, it aroused the people of Britain by the fervour of its campaign, fought the friends of Fascism in our midst and organised aid on behalf of the Spanish people. Members of its staff fought and died in the ranks of the International Brigade.

Our first loss was that talented young author and intellectual, Ralph Fox, who was killed at Cordova in January, 1937.[*] Fox, who had been in charge of the Worker's Notebook and was a regular contributor to the book page, was the author of a number of books and had a brilliant literary future before him. Although only a young man, he had already written a vivacious novel, *Storming Heaven,* a powerful historical study of Genghis Khan, a study of Lenin and two volumes on *Class Struggles in*

.....................................................

[*] Fox had actually died in the Battle of Lopera, Jaén province, in December, 1936, but his death was not made public until the following month.—J.E.

*Britain.* His essay in Marxist criticism, *The Novel and the People,* was published after his death. Moving tributes were paid to him at a big mass meeting in London.

W.C. Rowney, our cartoonist Maro, to whom I have already referred, fell the next month, and in the next year we lost during the Aragon retreat in April two comrades, George Hardy, a machine-minder on our printers' jobbing side, and Walter Tapsell, known far and wide as "Tappie," who had been our general manager. "Tappie," who had a great reputation for Cockney wit and exuberance, was a close personal friend of mine and I felt his death very severely. I was in Spain at the time as the correspondent of the *Daily Worker,* and I shall never forget that day when I travelled to the front to find the British battalion in retreat and was told that "Tappie" was numbered among the missing. For over a month I searched the hospitals in the hope that he had been picked up wounded, but in the end was forced to the conclusion that he had been murdered by the Fascists. "Tappie" was the political commissar of the British Battalion and the Fascists always murdered commissars who fell into their hands.

The reporting by the *Daily Worker* of the Spanish war was exemplary. Only a few days after the Franco landings in the South, Frank Pitcairn was reporting events from Barcelona where the Fascists had been defeated and the people were in control of the city. Pitcairn fought as a militiaman in Madrid and remained in Spain for over a year. I followed his trail and was later succeeded by Peter Kerrigan. Sam Russell wound up the job.

During my time in Spain, the British Battalion was visited by a Labour delegation consisting of Mr. Attlee, Mr. Noel Baker and Miss Ellen Wilkinson. It was a memorable occasion and a hearty welcome was extended by the British fighters to their visitors. Ellen Wilkinson was much moved by her experiences and at one point burst into tears and cried out: "What can I do for you men?" Back came the answer: "Send us some Woodbines!" It was, of course, "Tappie's" voice. Drawn up on the village square at Mondejar in the falling darkness of a November evening, the British Battalion received the greetings of the Leader of the Labour Party and in return named its First Company the Major Attlee Company. Mr. Attlee expressed his pride in the honour conferred on him and left a message ending with the words, "Workers of the world unite!" No one thought then that some years later Mr. Attlee would form a Government which would maintain relations with Franco Spain and take steps to draw it into Western Union.

By August, 1936, the complicity of Hitler and Mussolini in the plot against Spanish democracy had been clearly established, but the Baldwin Government, with the support of the National Council of Labour, refused to lift a finger on behalf of Republican Spain and declared for a policy of neutrality. The *Daily Worker* replied with a denunciation of this policy as meaning a free hand for Hitler and Mussolini and carried day after day passionate appeals signed by Harry Pollitt calling for solidarity with the Republican Government and the abandonment of the deceptive neutrality policy.

The "non-intervention" agreement entered into by the Powers quickly proved to be a farce and, indeed, nothing but a cover for the supply of arms and men to Franco by Germany and Italy. On October 23, the Soviet Government denounced the violation of the agreement by a number of its participants and declared that the right to purchase arms abroad should be returned to the Spanish Government. The British Government refused to follow this lead. The National Council of Labour dropped its support for non-intervention, although no decision was taken to organise a mass campaign in support of the Spanish Republic.

The *Daily Worker* was now calling for "Arms for Spain" and Frank Pitcairn was reporting the presence of British volunteers in Spain. Some of these volunteers had been fighting in Spain since August and had taken part in the heroic defence of Madrid in November. By the end of December the British volunteers had been formed into a company, 145 strong, attached to the French Battalion, and went into action at Cordova. By the end of January, 1937, the British Battalion, now numbering six hundred, was organised and ready for action.

On January 11, 1937, the *Daily Worker* bitterly denounced the Government decision to enforce the Foreign Enlistment Act of 1870 and to place a ban on the departure of volunteers for Spain. The ban was, of course, ineffective. Later, Frank Pitcairn, who was back in London for a short period, was refused permission by the Foreign Office to return to Spain on the grounds that he had previously served as a volunteer. Mr. Attlee protested in the House of Commons, but the ban was maintained. Pitcairn, however, calmly took himself off and was soon in Madrid again; from there he telephoned a summing up of the situation. Announcing that he had gone without any endorsement on his passport, the *Daily Worker* declared that the presence of Frank Pitcairn in Madrid "is not merely the return of a foreign correspondent to his work, but the assertion by the *Daily Worker* and by Frank Pitcairn of the freedom of the Press, of the right of newspapermen to carry on their work unhindered by Government opposition, and of the liberty of a British citizen to travel freely abroad."

And so the battle went on. The *Daily Worker* waged it with argument, fact and appeal. It convinced the British people that non-intervention was a fraud and a sham; it helped to organise great mass demonstrations of solidarity with the Spanish Republicans; it explained that Spain was a rehearsal for the world war which the Nazis were preparing; it opened its columns to the appeals for the Dependants' Aid Fund of the International Brigade. The *Daily Worker* never relaxed its fight for Republican Spain and never will relax it until democracy again triumphs in that cruelly tortured country.

The coming to power of Hitler and the lessons of the struggle in Spain gave a strong impetus to united front activity in Britain and many Liberals and middle-class people were drawn into co-operation with Communists against Fascism. Even Mr. A.J. Cummings, of the *News Chronicle,* was announced as speaking at a Lenin Memorial meeting in 1936. But he didn't turn up!

Within the Labour movement the turn to unity was marked

by the coming together of the I.L.P., the Communist Party and the Socialist League, then affiliated to the Labour Party and headed by Sir Stafford Cripps. On January 18, 1937, the *Daily Worker* published a manifesto signed by the leaders of the three organisations which contained a programme of immediate demands which declared that "to weld the power of the workers into an unbreakable front, to advance in the fight for Socialism, we must mobilise for immediate objectives, clear in their appeal and vital in the battle against reaction and Fascism." This move was promptly supported by Professor Laski.* Throughout the country a number of mass demonstrations were organised in support of the Unity Campaign as it was called. The reply of Transport House† was the immediate disaffiliation of the Socialist League. Later, both Aneurin Bevan and G.R. Strauss‡ gave their support to the Unity Campaign.

These were the days when some of those people who today are the sworn enemies of the *Daily Worker* and its policy were contributing to our columns and had nothing but praise for the paper. In April, 1937, for example, Victor Gollancz, who now hob-nobs with Churchill, wrote an article on "Why I Read the *Daily Worker*." He said: "… the essence and importance of the

......................................

* Harold Laski, a Marxist economist and political theorist, and professor of political science at the London School of Economics.—J.E.

† Then Labour Party headquarters.—J.E.

‡ George Strauss, then M.P. for Lambeth North and later a minister in Clement Attlee's post-war Labour government.—J.E.

*Daily Worker* is precisely that it is the paper of the masses ... I mean that in more than the obvious sense; I mean that in its directness, its going straight to the point, its absence of humbug and artificiality and bogusness, it is characteristic of men and women, as opposed to ladies and gentlemen ... there is a certain solidity, a certain respect for intelligence, which is sadly lacking in almost every other paper I know." On these remarks we need make only one comment. The *Daily Worker* has not changed.

During this period the *Daily Worker* made solid progress and on its seventh birthday received warm greetings from, among others, Professor Laski, Low, Ebby Edwards, then secretary of the Miners' Federation of Great Britain, and Hamilton Fyfe.* How popular we were in those days! Fyfe wished us a two million circulation; Low said he preferred our sober statesmanship to the pernicious doctrines of propaganda sheets like *The Times;* Laski declared that we were necessary for the working class, and Edwards greeted the magnificent work we were doing for the working class and the miners in particular. I can only repeat that *we* have not changed.

But the *Daily Herald* begrudged our success and revamped the hoary lies about Moscow Gold in spite of the fact that we had raised no less than £33,950 in six years. In July, 1936, the *Herald* published an article headed "Communist Secrecy on Sources

......................................

* "Low" was the political cartoonist David Low; Hamilton Fyfe was a journalist who worked on the *Daily Mail* before editing the *Morning Advertiser, Daily Mirror* and *Daily Herald,* now the *Sun.*—J.E.

of Funds," in which it implied that the *Daily Worker* could not continue publication unless it was in receipt of subsidies from abroad. We got rather bored by this propaganda but it is regularly served up even to this day.

Our enemies have never been able to understand the finances of the *Daily Worker,* which appeared to them to be conducted in defiance of all the rules. Obviously, our advertising revenue was very low—only during this Popular Front period did we begin to get some steady revenue from this source, chiefly in the form of co-operative society advertisers, some publishers and a few private firms. Our circulation, which during the pre-war years never rose higher than 50,000 a day and 100,000 at week-ends, gave us an income that could be readily calculated. It was not very much.

We made both ends meet, nevertheless; not only through the medium of the Fighting Fund, but by a strict businesslike approach on all questions and by a régime of strict economy. We paid trade union rates of pay in all departments, but we did our utmost to keep the size of our staffs down and, in the case of the editorial, we worked miracles on the basis of an amazingly small expenditure.

On those occasions when we were faced with the necessity of raising new capital we resorted to special methods as, for example, when Printing Properties, Ltd., was formed as the holding company for the new plant and premises in Cayton Street. This company issued debentures which were taken up by a variety of people. Sir Stafford Cripps holds a debenture for

£50 and is likely to continue holding it for some time ahead unless his Government changes its policy. The explanation of Cripps' continued financial association with the Communists is simple. When our Cayton Street premises were destroyed by enemy action in April, 1941, Printing Properties, Ltd., were compelled to place themselves in the hands of a receiver and the debenture holders who, because of a change in political views, want their money back can do no more than whistle for it until the Government decides to pay out war damage compensation on such properties.

The particular advantage of such a holding company was that the company which published the *Daily Worker* did not own any plant or premises, but merely rented them. Therefore, evilly-intentioned persons who wanted to seize our assets through the medium of libel actions were not able to lay their hands on them as legally we possessed nothing except our ready cash and office furniture. And even this was safeguarded by the action of the directors of the publishing company who would sell their shares to a new company during the course of the given libel case. Prosecuting counsel, with a note of both sadness and sourness in their voices, would sometimes draw the attention of judges to these reprehensible practices of ours. But if the libel laws can be used for the penalisation of political opinion, I see no reason why the Companies Act should not be used to escape the consequences of the partisan application of the libel laws.

And to this I ought to add that we have never wilfully sought prosecution or persecution and, not being addicted to the habit of tilting at windmills, we have never set out to defy Britain's onerous set of libel laws. In point of fact, our aim has always been to keep the paper out of the courts as we expect nothing but short shrift when dragged before them. Not a line is ever published until it has passed under the eagle eye of our lawyers. Many are the arguments between these luckless individuals and the members of the editorial staff on how near the bone they can go in telling the truth or expressing an opinion on this or that matter! But in our hearts we are very grateful to our legal advisers who exercise a steadying effect upon the journalists and make them write with care and due attention to fact, time, place and circumstances.

During this period we acquired the services of two of our most famous contributors—Professor J.B.S. Haldane and Gabriel. Their talents are poles apart but each in his own way plays an outstanding part on the paper. Haldane's first article appeared on December 9, 1937, and was entitled "What Makes the Birth Rate Fall?" All through these years he has written weekly scientific articles for the paper with very few breaks. It is a great achievement and a proof that his profound scientific knowledge is combined with a rare journalistic skill and agility. Without doubt, Haldane's articles are our most popular feature, and even though some of them demand some hard thinking and concentration to grasp, they are eagerly sought after.

To great numbers of people, Haldane's name spells science not in an ivory tower but closely connected with the problems of the masses and their search for knowledge. He wants to help all of

RIDING DOWN THE SUNSET TRAIL.

A Gabriel cartoon from May 27 1936 on the resignation of J.H. Thomas
for giving away the government's Budget secrets to wealthy businessmen

us to understand the world and to use the scientific method in
politics. He possesses a great brain and also a natural humility. As
the chairman of our Editorial Board, Haldane exercises a strong
influence on the general approach of the paper; he is impatient
should we get our facts wrong and he is insistent on fairness and
balanced reporting. If the *Daily Worker* had done nothing more
than introduce science to the masses through the medium of the
Haldane articles, this would constitute in itself an achievement of
no mean significance. These articles have shown the educational
rôle that a paper can fulfil and it is a sad reflection on the state
of the Press that no other newspaper, not even *The Times,* makes
it a regular policy to publish articles of this character.

Gabriel first appeared on the scene in February, 1936. In him there was immediately recognised an artist with a sure political understanding. Both his artistic and political "line" were just what we were waiting for! Apart from being a cartoonist, Gabriel is also a writer and critic of considerable talent. Gabriel has had many outstanding successes and his books of collected cartoons have had a wide sale. During his beginner's period on the paper, we were particularly fond of his cartoon on the resignation of J.H. Thomas following that gentleman's betrayal of the Budget secrets.* It was entitled "Riding Down the Sunset Trail," and portrayed the notorious Right Honourable Dress Shirt mounted on an old hack and sadly leaving Uncle Stan Baldwin in his old shack.

Gabriel also drew several striking cartoons on the King Edward-Mrs. Simpson affair which culminated in the abdication of the King on December 10, 1936. His crowning effort was a portrayal of Baldwin as a king-eating lion with a caption in the form of verses with apologies to Stanley Holloway. The *Daily Worker* comment on this affair was forthright and in keeping with its republican tradition. It wrote:

"The ruling financial oligarchy, represented by Baldwin, has driven out one royal figurehead, who did not suit them,

.................................................

* Jimmy Thomas, former National Union of Railwaymen leader and Secretary of State for the Colonies in the National Government until he was found guilty of passing Budget secrets to his stockbroker son Leslie, Tory M.P. Sir Alfred Butt and wealthy businessman Alfred "Cosher" Bates.—J.E.

" Now young Edward had heard about lions,
How they were ferocious and wild,
And to see Stanley lying so peaceful
Didn't seem right to the child.

" So straightaway the brave little fellow,
Not showing a morsel of fear,
Took his stick with the Royal Arms on the handle
And poked it in Stanley's rear.

" You could see that the lion didn't like it,
For giving a kind of a roar,
He pulled young Edward inside the cage with him
And swallowed the little chap whole.

" The family said ' Yon lion's eaten our Edward,
And him about to get married next day !'
They were asked ' How much to settle the matter ?'
The answer is ' How much do you usually pay ? '."
(With apologies to Stanley Holloway.)

Gabriel's cartoon from December 12, 1936 on the abdication of King
Edward VIII at the behest of Stanley Baldwin and his government

to put another more pliable one in his place. Is this a victory for democracy? No. The forces associated with Baldwin
are the reactionary ruling forces of British monopoly capital, the enemies of democracy throughout the world …
All the sanctimonious moral and constitutional arguments
which have been put forward by Baldwin and accepted at
face value by the chiefs of the Labour Party, are only the
cover for the real aim. Their real aim is to strengthen the
Monarchy as the tool of reaction against democracy, against
Socialism, against the colonial peoples."

A small taste of the *Daily Worker's* coverage of the Battle of Cable Street: above left, a montage of photos and sketches from the demonstration; above right, part of the Saturday supplement calling for a massive turnout to stop Mosley; opposite, the front page proclaiming victory

At this time the *Daily Worker* was conducting a powerful and systematic campaign against the ever-increasing activities of the Mosley gang of Fascists who were endeavouring to drive their activities into the working-class areas of the East End for the purpose of stirring up anti-Semitic conflict. The culminating point came on October 4, 1936, when Mosley organised a march into the East End in the form of a military operation. The *Daily Worker* answered with a call to the London workers to action under the rallying slogan of "They shall not pass!" And, indeed, the Fascists did not pass eastward, they were routed and com-

pelled to make a bedraggled return westward.

On Saturday, October 3, the *Daily Worker* came out with twelve pages, including a special four-page supplement entirely devoted to the story of the people's fight against Fascism. The response was enormous and it is estimated that a quarter of a million people answered the call and gathered at Aldgate and Cable Street. In Cable Street itself barricades were thrown up. The masses supported the policy of the Communist Party, namely, to clear the Fascists off the streets, and they ignored the advice of the Labour Party which told them to stay indoors. The final result was that the police, who were present in vast numbers, banned the march after fruitless efforts to get the Fascists through. The people had won the day.

The comments afterwards are worth recording. Said Mosley: "The leader of the British Union of Fascists places on record the fact that this is the first occasion on which the British Government has openly surrendered to Red Terror." Scotland Yard issued the following highly comical effort: "A Fascist assembly was held in the East End today, and largely owing to one of the finest days of the year, many people were attracted to it, including a large number of women and children." The *Daily Worker* said: "The workers of London have won a tremendous victory. Mosley said he would march his militaristic columns through the East End. The police said Yes; the Home Secretary said Yes; the Cabinet said Yes; but the workers said NO! And NO it was."

As the Fascists had no love for the *Daily Worker,* our premises had to be carefully protected against their playful habits of damaging property and beating up their opponents.* One such incident took place on the night of January 21, 1936, when a gang of about 30 Fascists gathered in Cayton Street carrying milk bottles and rubber truncheons and shouting "Down with the Yids" and "It's an insult to the King." They damaged two cars and broke a window with a milk bottle and then ran off. They were

........................................

* At the end of 1934, shortly before our move to Cayton Street, a small gang of Fascists burst into the warehouse of our printer's late at night, beat up the paper's night publisher, and damaged some equipment. Arrested and sentenced to varying terms of imprisonment by the Old Street magistrate, they got the sentences quashed on appeal to London Sessions.

recognised as notorious Fascist characters from Shoreditch.

One year after his East End fiasco, on October 3, 1937, Mosley tried another march into a working-class area, this time into Bermondsey. He was again answered by the *Daily Worker* and the Communist Party. Heavily protected by thousands of foot and mounted police who repeatedly charged the protesting workers, Mosley marched his 2,000 followers into Bermondsey but failed to reach the meeting place he had planned. The police finally succeeded in protecting him by cordoning off a wide network of side streets and no one except his own marchers was allowed within hearing distance.

In June, 1937, the *Daily Worker* found itself before the courts again arising from its publication of certain correspondence belonging to the Economic League which had fallen into its hands. Sir Walter Citrine was hot on our trail in connection with these letters and succeeded in getting £500 out of us as damages for libel. The Economic League, as is well known, is an organisation formed by a number of big employers for the purpose of carrying on propaganda, especially in the factories and trade unions, against the aims and objects of the Labour movement. In charge of its Lancashire and Cheshire district was a certain Major R.R. Hoare, who happened to enjoy the distinction of being the cousin of Sir Samuel Hoare, now Lord Templewood. The letters in question were those which had passed between Major Hoare and the director of the Economic League, Mr. J. Baker White, now Tory M.P. for Canterbury.

These letters were indeed amazing because they revealed that

Mr. Baker White was boasting to Major Hoare of his contacts with Labour leaders, of his help to the Labour Party in its fight against Communism, and of his ability to supply employers with information regarding the activities of "extremists" among the workers. On the other hand, Major Hoare was boasting to Mr. Baker White of his co-operation with the Manchester and Salford Police Forces in the collection of information regarding trade union and Communist activities. A memorandum from the gallant major to a certain Detective Eckersley read as follows: "I understand that there will probably be a meeting of the executive of the unofficial shop stewards' movement at the Albion Hotel on Thursday next at 7.45 p.m. Can you get this meeting covered as I consider it of considerable importance?"

The publication of these letters caused a great sensation. But then followed the court actions. The Economic League applied for an injunction to prevent the *Daily Worker* from using the letters with the result that the judge ordered the *Daily Worker* to give up all copies and to cease from giving them further publicity. The case for the paper was put by Sir Stafford Cripps, who argued that the Economic League was not entitled to the protection of the court as the letters were evidence of a criminal offence insofar as they proved that the police had been communicating information to outside persons without authority. He was, however, overruled by Mr. Justice Luxmoore, who said that there was no suggestion that the information given by the Manchester Police had been imparted in an unauthorised manner.

When Sir Walter's libel case against the *Daily Worker* came into court, we were compelled to make an apology and to pay him £500 and costs because his case was based on the claim that he had never had any kind of connection with Mr. Baker White of the Economic League, and that he had received an assurance from that gentleman that the letter as published in the *Daily Worker* was not a true copy of the letter which he, Mr. White, had sent to Major Hoare.

The letter we published asserted that "It may interest you to know that the co-operation between Sir Walter Citrine and myself on this question is far closer than most people imagine …" But Sir Walter's counsel stated in court that the copy of the letter produced by the Economic League showed that "in fact no such statements had been made and that what Mr. Baker White had stated was that in his opinion (and it was on erroneous information) the views of Sir Walter Citrine and the League might be found to be not very far apart."

Despite our mystification, what could we do in face of the Baker White affirmations? We had to apologise and submit to the ruling of the court. Following the hearing the *Daily Worker* published a statement that "in the present case Sir Walter Citrine denies that he was associated with the Economic League in any way, and we have accepted the denial and apologised for it. But that is the extent of our admission and the apology."

During these two years, 1936-7, the war policies of the aggressive Powers, Germany, Italy and Japan, began to take full shape and were connived at and assisted by the so-called democratic

Powers. Following the introduction of conscription, Hitler marched into the demilitarised zone of the Rhineland in defiance of the Locarno Pact and Versailles Treaty on March 7, 1936. There was grave alarm in France but secret joy in the leading circles of the Conservative Government in London. Hitler was still talking peace and the *Daily Herald* expressed its belief in the sincerity of Hitler's offer of a non-aggression pact. The *Daily Worker's* leading article on these events was clear and incisive:

"Those who are spreading illusions about Hitler's 'peace' gesture, and who urge that his proposals should be accepted, are aiding the war plans of Baldwin. Whatever their motives, Mr. George Lansbury and those Liberal pacifists who are reaching out to grasp Hitler's 'olive branch' are, in fact, giving support to the policy of war on the Soviet Union ... It must never be forgotten that it is this National Government that has made it possible for Hitler Fascism to become a menace to the peace of the world. It was the Baldwin Government which encouraged Hitler's war plans against the Soviet Union. It was the Bank of England which supplied the money for German rearmament. It was the Baldwin Government which refused to give an assurance of support to France against Hitler's military aggression."

The aggressors were, moreover, drawing still closer together for common action. In November, 1936, the Rome-Berlin axis was followed up by the signing by Germany and Japan of the Anti-Comintern Pact, described by the *Daily Worker* as directed against "collective security, the League of Nations and the democratic countries." This was the signal to Japan to launch, in the following year, a new attack on Central China and to occupy Shanghai.

The *Daily Worker* unceasingly explained precisely what was happening in the world, that the rape of Abyssinia, followed by the occupation of the Rhineland, the intervention against Republican Spain and the new attack on China all meant that the aggressors had seized the initiative, that they were being encouraged by the policy of British imperialism and that the outbreak of a second world war was drawing nearer.

It is true that millions of people became alarmed and that the forces of the Popular Front were growing, but within the ranks of the Labour movement there was the utmost confusion and division. The Right Wing were, in fact, secretly supporting the Baldwin policy although they frequently resorted to pacifist phrases and to belated expressions of opposition. The *Daily Herald* persistently attributed the best of intentions to Hitler and the half-hearted opposition to non-intervention in Spain was adopted only after a preliminary period of support.

In the course of constant articles the *Daily Worker* did its utmost to clarify these issues, many of which came under discussion at the notorious Edinburgh Conference of the Labour Party in October, 1936, which passed an unclear resolution on armaments and attacked the international policy of the Baldwin Government, although its Parliamentary leaders were in practice supporting it. Summing up the results of this conference, the

*Daily Worker* reported Harry Pollitt as saying:

"It put forward a policy on every urgent issue which was not merely ambiguous and unconvincing, but reactionary and dangerous to the whole future of the working-class movement. The majority of the delegates have come home disturbed, dissatisfied and confused, and feeling that the present Labour Party leadership is operating a policy that means surrender to the National Government. Make no mistake, the Labour leaders know what they want and the confusion and doubt of the Edinburgh Conference is one of the processes by which they carry into practice their policy."

These were harsh words but they were amply justified by the events of that year and received further justification when the dread story of the defeat of the Spanish Republic, the seizure of Austria, the betrayal at Munich, the invasion of Czechoslovakia and the sabotage of the Anglo-Soviet negotiations unfolded itself in the three subsequent years.

Since its entry into the League of Nations with the object of hindering the outbreak of war, the Soviet Union had played an increasing part in international affairs in order to strengthen the front against aggression. On March 18, 1936, the *Daily Worker* reported at length the speech delivered by the Soviet representative, Litvinov, before the Council of the League of Nations on the Hitler occupation of the Rhineland. It was a masterly indictment of Fascism and a call to the other Powers to act in a spirit of collective security. But as is well known it fell on deaf ears precisely because the other leading Powers in the League were more concerned with encouraging Hitler to attack in the East than they were with stopping him in the West.

The rest of the British Press was in no way interested in supporting the stand taken by the Soviet Union or in advocating policies that would facilitate the conclusion of the Anglo-Soviet Alliance which in 1941 was to become the corner-stone of our defence against Fascism. Fleet Street continued to publish fantastic stories about life in the Soviet Union, and when the famous Moscow trials began the British newspapers from *The Times* to the *Mirror* poured ridicule and scorn on the proceedings and entirely failed to understand that the Soviet Government was taking vital measures to root out the traitors in preparation for the years of trial that it could see ahead.

Following the celebrated trial of Marshal Tukhachevsky and the seven generals associated with him which took place in June, 1936, the *Daily Herald* immediately took the accused to heart, treated the whole affair as a mystery, howled about the dark cloud of a "reign of terror" in the Soviet Union, and treated the trial as an attempt on the part of the "bureaucracy" to get rid of those who "have dared to murmur against its dictates." In just another three years the *Daily Herald* was presented with tangible proof, in the shape of the Fifth Column in France, of the extent of the Nazi spy machine and the depths of its intrigue. If only the French traitors had been despatched with the same swift and timely justice that was meted out to Tukhachevsky and his gang!

It is a tragic thought to recall that during those vital years leading up to the war the hysteria created by the Press made it practically impossible to obtain a dispassionate hearing for the proposal that Britain and the Soviet Union should consider the question of common action against Hitler. In those years the Press lords were very fond of the Nazis primarily because they regarded them as a means of crushing Communism. Fleet Street hated Communism much more than it did Fascism.

## Chapter Five
# The Year of Munich

IN THE TWO years immediately preceding the outbreak of the war, the economic situation in Britain had again worsened following the improvement which had begun in 1935. Both the cost of living and the figures of unemployment were rising again and the pernicious means test was being imposed. The figures for December, 1937, showed an increase of 166,204 on the previous month and by January had nearly reached the two million mark again. The *Daily Worker,* as usual, was backing the struggle of the unemployed and doing its best on the strike front.

With the opening of 1938, the *Daily Worker* ran several interviews on the possibilities of a new slump and received a message from Sir Stafford Cripps which ended with the declaration that we must go forward until we "sweep from power the ruling classes and place in their seats the trusted representatives of the workers." Ten years later Sir Stafford was telling the astonished British workers that they were not fit to run industry and the *Economist* was writing that "there is nothing inherently impossible in the conception of a Left government pursuing Right policies; that is what Sir Stafford Cripps has been doing for the last twelve months." When it comes to political somersaults, the Communists look mere amateurs compared to these accomplished acrobats.

This was the decisive year of Munich when the Tory policy of strengthening Hitler with the hope of provoking war between Germany and the Soviet Union reached its culminating point and made the second world war inevitable. The *Daily Worker* maintained its unswerving policy of opposition to Fascism and fought day in and day out for Republican Spain. But the rest of the Press, with certain honourable exceptions, established close relations with the Nazis and played Hitler's game.

Light on what was proceeding behind the scenes was thrown by Mr. Wickham Steed, a former editor of *The Times,* in his Penguin, *The Press,* which was published on November 11, 1938. In a postscript prepared the previous month he wrote:

"Since these lines were written in mid-September the British Press has—with one or two notable exceptions—made further progress on the road that leads to totalitarian servitude ... On the early afternoon of Sunday, October 9, the German Dictator, Herr Hitler, fortified by the Munich Agreement and by the scrap of paper which he and the British Prime Minister had signed ... on pain of German displeasure placed his veto on the return to office of three prominent British public men. (Hitler's reference was to Eden, Churchill and Duff Cooper.) When this news was broadcast on the evening of Sunday, October 9, the whole nation was moved to wrath. Of the depth of its wrath hardly a hint was given the next morning in the leading

British newspapers, some of which were almost apologetic. Inquiry into this humiliating behaviour on the part of our 'free Press' elicited the information that certain large advertising agents had warned journals for which they provide much revenue that advertisements would be withheld from them should they play up the international crisis and cause an alarm which was 'bad for trade.' None of the newspapers thus warned dared to publish the names of these advertising agents or hold them up to public contempt.... During the international crisis the majority of our newspapers toned down the news and withheld frank comment upon it. This they did partly in response to suggestions 'confidentially' made by some clandestine organisation that represents, or pretends to represent, the views of official quarters."

The reader will notice that these revelations by Mr. Wickham Steed fit closely with the statements quoted from Mr. Francis Williams in Chapter I (p.28-9) on how Sir Samuel Hoare arranged the handling of the Press during that period.

More information was recently forthcoming in German documents published by the Soviet Government. On May 6, 1938, von Dirksen, the German Ambassador in London, wrote to the editor of the *Daily Mail,* thanking him "very sincerely" for his courtesy in submitting before publication an article by Lord Rothermere entitled "Postscripts" which, among other things, said that "Czechoslovakia is not of the remotest concern to us. If France likes to burn her fingers there it is a matter for France." Another document reports Dirksen informing Berlin that "the historian, Sir Raymond Beazley, advised by the Embassy, regularly sends letters to influential provincial papers."

Our Press lords, particularly Lord Kemsley,* appeared greatly impressed by the gangsters who were leading the Nazi Party. Kemsley, who visited Hitler in the summer of 1939 and offered to give space to the Nazi point of view in his newspapers, is reported by von Dirksen as having spoken "with pleasure of his conversation with Reichsleiter Rosenberg (charming personality). He was strongly impressed by the personality of Reichsminister Goebbels, whom he thought a clever and broadly educated man."

Then we get a picture of von Dirksen and Sir Horace Wilson[†] discussing how to hoodwink the British public. One month before the outbreak of the war these two beauties had a discussion, and according to von Dirksen: "Wilson pointed out that in England confidence in Germany and her peaceful intentions had been shattered; the thing above all was to teach the British public that confidence was warranted." No approaches were made to the *Daily Worker!*

The first major political event of 1938 which brought the real meaning of the Government's foreign policy out into the open

---

* His Kemsley Newspapers owned a string of right-wing publications including the *Daily Telegraph, Sunday Graphic* and *Daily Sketch,* which later merged with the *Daily Mail.*—J.E.

† A long-serving civil servant who by this time was an influential adviser to Neville Chamberlain—and was widely reviled for his behind-the-scenes part in appeasement.—J.E.

and revealed the split in the Tory Party was the resignation of Eden from the Foreign Secretaryship on February 21. This was done in a very restrained and gentlemanly manner and Eden made no attempt to indict the Chamberlain policy as pro-Fascist and a betrayal of Britain's national interests. He was promptly succeeded at the Foreign Office by Lord Halifax.

In his book, *The Gathering Storm,* Churchill has told us of his emotional reaction to the resignation of his young friend: "From midnight to dawn I lay in my bed consumed by emotions of sorrow and fear. There seemed one strong, young figure standing up against long, dismal, drawling tides of drift and surrender, of wrong measurements and feeble impulses.... Now he was gone. I watched the daylight slowly creep in through the windows, and saw before me in mental gaze the vision of Death." The *Daily Worker* felt quite differently about the resignation of Eden for it saw in this division in the National Government the opportunity for the Labour Party to rally the masses for a peace policy. In a specially displayed article, R. Palme Dutt wrote:

"Eden's resignation has placed the whole political situation in the hands of the people of this country. The Labour Party and all supporters of peace have it now in their power by a swift and combined offensive to smash this rump Cabinet of agents of Hitler and Mussolini. Either Britain in the hands of the Chamberlains and Halifaxes is henceforth to be the servile ally and tool of Hitler and Mussolini, an integral part of the Fascist bloc, the fourth wheel in the coach of the Triple Pact of Fascist murderers

HIS MAJESTY'S FOREIGN SECRETARIES

Gabriel's response on February 23, 1938, to the resignation of Anthony Eden and the Chamberlain government's policy of appeasement

and warmakers, with all that this will mean in war abroad and slavery at home. Or the people of Britain can defeat this foul conspiracy, and range Britain once and for all with the democracies of the world for the victory of peace."

Gabriel produced one of his most brilliant cartoons, captioned "His Majesty's Foreign Secretaries," which depicted Hitler and Mussolini marching into 10 Downing Street with Chamberlain and other members of the Cabinet on their knees giving the Nazi salute. There was not the slightest doubt that Chamberlain was very glad to shift Eden, whose resignation was regarded by Mussolini as a personal triumph for himself. It paved the way for the reaching of an understanding between Chamberlain and Mussolini and for the signing two months later of the Anglo-Italian Agreement, which finally abandoned Spain to the Fascist invaders.

Nearly ten years were to pass before details of the inside story of the events preceding the resignation of Eden were to be revealed to the world. According to the report of the Italian Ambassador in London to his Foreign Secretary, Count Grandi, included in *Ciano's Diplomatic Papers,* published in December, 1948, Chamberlain was maintaining private contact with the Ambassador through a "confidential agent" and discussing matters behind Eden's back. In his report dated February 19, 1938, the Ambassador tells of a discussion with Chamberlain at which Eden was also present. From the whole trend of the recorded conversation it is clear that Chamberlain was seeking arguments from the Italian in order to confound Eden who was then standing out against the proposed Anglo-Italian Agreement. The Ambassador reports:

"Certainly this discussion of yesterday was one of the most paradoxical and extraordinary in which it has been my lot to take part ... The questions and queries addressed to me by Chamberlain were all, without exception, intentionally put with the aim of producing replies which would have the effect of contradicting and overthrowing the basis of argument on which Eden had evidently previously constructed, or by which he had attempted to justify, his miserable anti-Italian and anti-Fascist policy in opposition to Chamberlain and before his colleagues in the Cabinet ... Chamberlain, in fact, in addressing his questions directly to me, expected from me—this was obvious—nothing more or less than those details and definite answers which were useful to him as ammunition against Eden ... Purely as a matter of historical interest, I inform Your Excellency that yesterday evening after the Downing Street meeting, Chamberlain secretly sent his agent to me (we made an appointment in an ordinary public taxi) to say that he 'sent me cordial greetings, that he had appreciated my statements, which had been very useful to him, and that he was confident that everything would go very well next day.'"

Such a man was that Chamberlain who guided Britain's fortunes during those fateful years, a Prime Minister who did not disdain to intrigue with the Fascists against his own Foreign Secretary.

The *Daily Worker,* of course, had no knowledge of these Cabinet secrets in those days, although it knew sufficient of Chamberlain's policy to denounce him as a miserable agent of Hitler and Mussolini. This dispatch of the Italian Ambassador fully justifies the attitude of the *Daily Worker* to the crisis provoked by the Eden resignation and also its criticism directed against the weak-kneed attitude taken up by Chamberlain himself.

A special meeting of the joint executives of the Labour Party, Parliamentary Labour Party and Trades Union Congress issued a strong manifesto condemning "the weakness and cowardice" of the Government, demanding a stand against the violence and threats of the Fascist Powers and the calling of an immediate General Election. But no practical action was taken to back these words. Spain was still the crucial question but nothing was done to secure arms for Spain. The only aid rendered to Spain by the official Labour movement were words of sympathy and the collection of relief funds. This attitude of the Labour leaders to Spain is well summed up by G.D.H. Cole in his book, *A History of the Labour Party from 1914,* where he writes that "The official labour bodies did their best to salve the Labour movement's conscience by organising much needed relief measures and Red Cross services for the Spanish Republicans ... but it refused to inaugurate any national campaign in the Spanish cause."

On Friday, March 11, Hitler marched on Austria and that small country was quickly overwhelmed. Many crocodile tears were shed in the Press but everybody knew that Chamberlain had tacitly agreed to this further act of aggression and that the driving of Eden from office was one of the preparatory steps. Even then, several months before Munich, Chamberlain was already contemplating how the sacrifice of Czechoslovakia could be arranged. In his speech of March 14 on the Austrian events he failed to give any guarantees of British Government action should Hitler attack Czechoslovakia and noted with satisfaction that Goering had promised to improve German-Czech relations.

The Communist Party again approached the Labour Party urging united action and its letter was prominently featured in the *Daily Worker*. In the light of subsequent developments, Harry Pollitt's words have a prophetic ring about them:

"The German invasion of Austria is the first fruit of the infamous Chamberlain policy, which both parties have opposed. There is no need to tell your executive that it is only a first step. Tomorrow it will be Czechoslovakia and then France. The prospect of a Fascist Europe menaces the British people. Only one thing can prevent this—the action of the British people, and the only means of rousing every man and woman in Britain to demand this drastic change of policy, is the co-operation of all the Labour, Communist and democratic forces in Great Britain."

This appeal shared the fate of all other efforts. It was rejected; but the keen desire of the masses for action in defence of peace was, however, expressing itself in the movement and the campaign for a United Peace Alliance launched by *Reynolds News* aroused big support in the Co-operative movement. At its Easter Conference the Co-operative Party carried a resolution in favour of the Peace Alliance in spite of the opposition of Mr. A.V. Alexander.* The annual conference of the Shop Assistants' Union followed suit, and a couple of weeks later a similar resolution was carried at the annual conference of the National Union of Distributive and Allied Workers.

At this time I was reporting from Spain where the military situation had sadly deteriorated as a result of the Fascist

......................................................

* A prominent Co-operative Party M.P.—J.E.

breakthrough on the Aragon front. But the Republican troops were fighting well and the situation was by no means hopeless. On May 25 the *Daily Worker* published on its front page two dispatches from its special correspondents abroad, one from myself in Barcelona telling of the Republican recovery from its March defeat and the opening of an offensive in Catalonia, and the other from Frank Pitcairn in Prague reporting on the Nazi plans against the independence of Czechoslovakia. The meaning of Spain was well understood in Prague. "Tens of thousands of people are wearing little Spanish flags in their button-holes," reported Pitcairn.

During that heroic summer of 1938 our main attention was concentrated on the gathering war crisis, especially Hitler's plans for the seizure of Czechoslovakia. At the end of July the Japanese militarists decided on a try-out in the Far East against the Red Army and launched several attacks against Soviet territory at Lake Hasan near the Manchurian border. They were repulsed and driven out, but the incident assumed serious proportions and the Japanese would probably have tried further action if they had not been decisively defeated. The fighting at Lake Hasan was a warning of how far Hitler's allies in the Far East were prepared to go once the opportunity presented itself.

In Europe, attention was beginning to switch from Spain as Hitler began to spin his web around Czechoslovakia and the leaders of that country, some of them frightened and others plain treacherous, began their fatal retreat. The *Daily Worker* at no time had any illusions regarding the rôle of Czechoslovakia in

European affairs and the intentions of the Nazis. Day after day it indicted the policy of the Chamberlain Government as being an incitement to Hitler to pursue his policy of aggression.

When Chamberlain made it known that he was sending Lord Runciman to Prague as a "mediator and adviser," the *Daily Worker* raised a serious cry of alarm at the appointment of this cynical old Simonite Liberal. The *Daily Herald* wished him "good luck," but we declared: "We condemn this mission and we charge the Chamberlain Government with criminal interference in the internal affairs of a democratic country in the interests, not of peace and justice, but of its own imperialist plans to drive a bargain with the enemy."

All through August, Hitler continued to aggravate the international situation by stepping up the demands of the Sudeten Germans led by the Nazi Henlein. The Prague Government, under the influence of Runciman, made concession after concession, but they were of no avail. The situation was tense but the Chancellor of the Exchequer, Sir John Simon, made a speech saying that he had nothing to add to Chamberlain's March declaration that Britain could give no guarantee to go automatically to the assistance of Czechoslovakia should she be attacked. The *Daily Worker* reported Lloyd George's description of the Simon speech as "stale slosh."

On August 31, we reported that the Cabinet had decided that Chamberlain should write a "personal and friendly letter" to Hitler. This decision we pointed out really amounted to an offer to do a deal and our diplomatic correspondent referred to the possibility of "calling Hitler or his representatives to a conference, which would be intended to pave the way for an agreement between Chamberlain and the Nazis, parallel to the agreement between him and Mussolini." That was a pretty fair forecast of the subsequent turn of events except that it was Chamberlain who went to Hitler. On the same day the *Daily Worker* featured the three following demands in heavy black type on its front page:

"(1) The immediate recall of Parliament so that the voice of the British people shall be heard.

"(2) A categorical declaration from the National Government that it will immediately associate itself with France and the Soviet Union in whatever action they may take in the event of a German attack on the Czechoslovak Republic.

"(3) An immediate meeting of the National Council of Labour to plan national action to ensure that the people's desire for peace and strong action against the aggressors shall determine the policy of British democracy now and in the future."

Day by day the *Daily Worker* warned that all the concessions made by the Prague Government were merely whetting Hitler's appetite and that there existed a tacit understanding between Chamberlain and Hitler to compel the Czechoslovaks to give up without a struggle. On September 7, we wrote the following prophetic words: "Whatever positions Hitler gains will be used almost immediately as a jumping-off ground for a new attack, an attack which will find the democracies in a much worse position than they are at the moment. There may be 'peace' for a few days or a few weeks, and then Hitler will strike again. Then there WILL be war." In the same number we published an interview with Klement Gottwald, the leader of the Communist Party of Czechoslovakia who ten years later was to become the President of the Republic in succession to Dr. Benes. Gottwald told the *Daily Worker* that: "Hitler is not concerned with the solution of the Sudeten problem. That for him is a pretext upon which to destroy Czechoslovakia as an independent State. No concessions, however great, will be sufficient to make him leave Czechoslovakia in peace. Rights and bread for the German people, but no strategic positions for those who are preparing blows against the existence of our country."

*The Times,* under the influence of the Cliveden Set,* then entered the lists with a notorious "suggestion" that the Sudeten areas of Czechoslovakia should be ceded to Germany. This was the deal that Chamberlain was working for and which was finally sealed at the Munich Conference. With the ceding of these powerful defence areas to the Nazis the seizure of the whole of Czechoslovakia automatically followed a few months later. Thus the world war became inevitable. It followed less than one year after the signing of the Munich Pact.

..............................................

\* Claud Cockburn's name for a group of pro-Nazi aristocrats, politicians, businessmen and newspaper editors including Lord and Lady Astor (whose home gave the Set its name), Lord Halifax and *Times* editor Geoffrey Dawson.—J.E.

On September 15, Chamberlain flew off to Berchtesgaden and talked with Hitler for three hours. The man with the umbrella had begun his fatal last moves. It was his response to Hitler's sabre-rattling speech at Nuremberg. Chamberlain's aim was to reach agreement with Hitler at the expense of the Czechs and by bringing about a Czech surrender to nip in the bud the growing movement in favour of a stand against Hitler on the basis of joint action by Britain, France and the Soviet Union.

The policy of the Communist Party and the *Daily Worker* was that Hitler could be stopped by the unity of the democratic Powers and that his bluff could be called before the policy of retreat enabled him to become strong enough to declare war. On the other hand, Chamberlain and the Tories sought to delude the people that Hitler was ready to strike now, that only a policy of appeasement could stave off the war and also give Britain time to complete its defences.

The policy of the Labour leaders in this crisis expressed as usual a double-dealing attitude. Protests were made against the dangers of Chamberlain's policy, but no effective action was organised. At decisive moments, such as the flight to Berchtesgaden, confused and contradictory statements were made which had the effect of misleading the masses. At a later stage protests were made against the Munich policy but the right wing enthusiastically supported the opening stages.

In contrast to the *News Chronicle,* which warned that "a deal may be done that will finally betray democracy," the *Daily Herald* came out with an editorial headed: "Good Luck, Chamberlain!"

It claimed that "Mr. Chamberlain has taken not only a bold course, but one which will receive general support, and which must win the sympathy of opinion everywhere, irrespective of party opinion." Sir Walter Citrine commented that "the visit provides evidence to the whole world that Mr. Chamberlain is leaving no course unexplored to reach a peaceful settlement." Compared to these right-wing Labour fawners upon Chamberlain, the harsh, condemnatory remarks made by Churchill read like the words of a flaming democrat.

Eight years later the *Daily Worker* was able to make public a document which threw a flood of light on the state of the German military forces at the time of Munich and revealed that Hitler's policy was based on a colossal bluff in opposition to the considered views of his generals who wanted the attack on Czechoslovakia to be postponed to a later date. In September, 1946, an official document containing an account of the examination by Allied officials in Germany of General Halder, Chief of the German General Staff from 1938 to 1942, came into our possession. We published the document on September 12 and 13, 1946.

According to Halder, Germany at Munich time had only two armoured divisions and the German commanders charged with carrying out an eventual operation against Czechoslovakia "gave a most unfavourable verdict on German military prospects." Von Rundstedt was one of those. If the French came in (as they were by treaty bound to), General Halder considered the prospect for Germany "nothing less than catastrophic." Halder further recounted that the German generals had therefore decided to act "to prevent what they felt was inevitable catastrophe to Germany, by removing Hitler." The leaders of this conspiracy were Halder himself, von Witzleben, the commander of the Berlin garrison, General Becker, Halder's predecessor, Helldorf, Police President in Berlin, Graf Brockdorff, head of the Potsdam garrison, and Stuelpnagel.

Their plan was to arrest Hitler when he arrived in Berlin after leaving the Nuremberg Congress, but he proceeded to Berchtesgaden instead. On Tuesday, September 13, Hitler returned to Berlin and Halder decided to strike the next day. But the blow never fell as on that very evening of Wednesday, September 14, there was suddenly issued from 10 Downing Street the announcement that Mr. Chamberlain was flying to Berchtesgaden the next day to meet Hitler. The report of the interrogation continues:

"This involved the immediate dropping of the plan, since the prospect of war receded, and Halder, who was by no means a rebel by nature, felt that only the extreme necessity of preventing a major catastrophe could have justified him breaking his oath as a military officer. There was also a practical difficulty in that immediately on the receipt of this news Hitler flew back to Berchtesgaden and thus escaped their clutches. This extraordinary coincidence between the imminent execution of this operation and Chamberlain's visit may sound extremely theatrical but General Halder assured the interrogators it was fully in accordance with the facts. If Chamberlain had postponed his visit, or rather the announcement of his visit, by only a day, Hitler would have been deposed and the subsequent war prevented. 'But it was God's will, and God's ways are inscrutable,' added Halder."

Halder's account of the opposition of the German generals to an attack on Czechoslovakia in 1938 was confirmed by the proceedings at the Nuremberg trial. In a directive to Marshal von Keitel dated June 18, Hitler gave the following assurances: "I will decide to take action against Czechoslovakia only if I am firmly convinced, as in the case of the demilitarised zone and the entry into Austria, that France will not march, and that therefore England will not intervene." Take note also of the following extract from the Nuremberg proceedings: "Colonel Ecer, representing Czechoslovakia, asked Marshal Keitel: 'Would the Reich have attacked Czechoslovakia in 1938 if the Western Powers had stood by Prague?' Marshal Keitel: 'Certainly not. We were not strong enough militarily. The object of Munich was to get Russia out of Europe, to gain time, and to complete the German armaments.'"

In contrast to those apologists of Munich who claimed either that Chamberlain was deceived by Hitler's bluff or that he was deliberately playing for time in order to be able to strengthen Britain's defences, the *Daily Worker* took the view that Chamberlain was deliberately egging on Hitler to proceed with his war plans against the Soviet Union and well understood that the sacrifice of the Sudeten defence line would enormously strengthen Hitler's strategical position in Europe.

Those were tense days and events moved with amazing rapidity. On September 22, Chamberlain flew again to Hitler and met him at Godesberg. Chamberlain flew back the next day, and on September 27, on the eve of Parliament meeting, he made his notorious broadcast in which he referred to "a quarrel in a far-away country, between people of whom we know nothing."

This curious broadcast was a cunning mixture of peaceful self-righteousness and an attempt to stampede people into believing that the Government was desperately striving to preserve Britain from the imminent danger of war. Chamberlain referred to the digging of trenches and the trying on of gas masks at the orders of the Government as a regrettable necessity and he made a call for volunteers for A.R.P., the Fire Brigade and Territorials. Commented the *Daily Worker:* "The Chamberlain Government is aiming to create a war scare among the civilian population to get people to accept its policy of 'peace at any price' and enable more concessions to be given to Hitler."

The National Council of Labour put out strong declarations of opposition to Chamberlain's policy but the right wing, who had supported the Chamberlain flight to Berchtesgaden, did their utmost to sabotage the growing mass protest. Said Mr. Charles Dukes of the General Council of the Trades Union Congress: "We are in a crisis, and no matter who is in power we shall stand behind the Government. It is our Government and that is all that matters."

When the final test arrived on September 28 and Chamberlain

announced in the House of Commons his intention to fly to Munich to conclude an agreement with Hitler, Mussolini and Daladier over the dismembered body of Czechoslovakia, not a single protest came from Conservative, Labour, Liberal or I.L.P. Members. Only one Member of Parliament rose to denounce the scheme. It was William Gallacher, the solitary Communist. The situation was well summed up by a reader of the *Daily Worker* who wrote that "Chamberlain is the greatest statesman Germany ever had."

The other side of the Munich story which needs to be told is of the manoeuvres resorted to by Chamberlain in order to prevent the Soviet Union from having a say in the crisis. Three days before the final meeting at Munich, i.e., at the very moment when the deal with Hitler was being finally sewn up, the Foreign Office issued a statement that: "If, in spite of the efforts made by the British Prime Minister, a German attack is made upon Czechoslovakia, the immediate result must be that France will be bound to come to her assistance, and Great Britain and Russia will certainly stand by France."

Like all the trench-digging and the gas mask-fitting this statement was pure bluff. There was no intention on the part of the Foreign Office to form a united front between Britain, France and the Soviet Union against Nazi Germany. The purpose of the Munich Conference was to exclude the Soviet Union from having any say in the determination of policies for Europe and to form a war bloc against the Soviet Union.

On September 22, the *Daily Worker* played up the famous

speech of Litvinov, the Soviet Foreign Minister, at the Assembly of the League of Nations the previous day. Litvinov said:

"When, a few days before I left for Geneva, the French Government for the first time inquired as to our attitude in the event of an attack on Czechoslovakia, I gave in the name of my government the following perfectly clear and unambiguous reply: 'We intend to fulfil our obligations under the pact, and, together with France, to afford assistance to Czechoslovakia by the ways open to us. Our War Department is ready immediately to participate in a conference with representatives of the French and Czechoslovak War Departments, in order to discuss the measures appropriate to the moment.... It was necessary, however, to exhaust all means of averting an armed conflict, and we considered one such method to be an immediate consultation between the Great Powers of Europe and other interested States, in order if possible to decide on the terms of a collective *demarche*.'"

Two days later Litvinov met the British representatives at the League of Nations and again pressed for a meeting of the Big Powers. The British promised to put the proposal before Whitehall, but no reply was ever received. If Chamberlain had agreed to go into conference with the Soviet Union it would have meant the formation of an anti-Fascist front and a complete reversal of his pro-Hitler policy. For these reasons the Soviet proposals were ignored, but in deference to public opinion the Foreign Office issued its deceitful bulletin suggesting that common action with the Soviet Government was under consideration.

When Chamberlain flew back from Munich waving his piece of paper a great wave of relief swept Britain. Such was the effect of the deliberately worked-up war scare that the masses were temporarily deluded into believing that, but for the sacrifice of Czechoslovakia to Hitler, Britain would have been drawn into war. Later they were to realise that it was precisely the sacrifice of Czechoslovakia that speeded the Hitler aggression.

The year had been a difficult financial one for the paper and as early as April we were in such a plight that R. Palme Dutt, who was then editing the paper, had to make a very serious appeal to the readers. On April 23 he wrote:

> "During this period the *Daily Worker* has given over its columns to appeals for funds for Spain, for the Dependants' Aid Fund, and, in the last three months, for the Communist Crusade Fund. But the point has now been reached when the *Daily Worker* is compelled to appeal on its own behalf, if its whole future is not to be imperilled.... In order to establish the paper soundly we must have £2,000 by the end of May. Already £300 has been received in the Fund for April, so to make up the total amount we need £1,700 within the next five weeks."

By the end of May, however, the paper actually received £2,254. It was well over the target. The Fighting Fund was then set at £1,000 a month and an announcement was made regarding the management's plans for the purchase of a new rotary machine.

But our financial difficulties did not result in any weakening of our principles. We have always been sadly in need of advertising revenue, but we point blank refused the "Square Deal" advertisement offered by the railway companies who were then running a big campaign regarding their financial position. We published a counter-advertisement pointing out that 100,000 railwaymen got a wage below 50s. a week and ending with the slogan "Clear the Line of Parasites."

At the end of that year we were able to announce that during the nine years of our existence we had collected for the Fighting Fund no less than £52,671. But our enemies still spread their fairy stories about Moscow gold!

## Chapter Six

# Nineteen Thirty-nine

ONE HARDLY KNOWS how to begin the story of this tumultuous year of 1939 when great events tumbled over one another and situations rapidly changed. In September came the long threatened war. It was at that moment that I returned to the editorship of the paper and resumed the post which I had vacated seven years earlier.

During the opening months of the year, the *Daily Worker* had ridden forward on the crest of the anti-Fascist wave. Proudly the paper announced on April 22 that it had gained ten thousand new readers in the first three months of the year, that £3,700 had been contributed to the Fighting Fund in 16 weeks, and that the installation of the new Crabtree rotary machine was nearing completion. A bigger and better paper, with attractive new features, was foretold as from May 1.

For on this day the new rotary went into action amid scenes of great jubilation. It was truly a red-letter day in the history of the paper, a triumph made possible by the confidence and courage of those responsible for the direction of the paper and the generous self-sacrifice of those who read it, distributed it and supported the cause it upheld. On May 2, Harry Pollitt described the scene when the new rotary moved into action in an article entitled "My Biggest Thrill":

"I have had my biggest thrill of all—one that brought pride, joy and a new kind of excitement to those who were privileged to see it. It was the new Crabtree rotary that is going to make such a tremendous difference to the *Daily Worker*. As I stood there, watching what the workers' pennies and shillings have helped us to purchase, I got a feeling that money can never buy. Off it goes! We watch and wait, but there are no flaws here. The great machine responds like clockwork. The *Daily Worker* comes through pile upon pile, to supply the needs of a record issue."

In those days, almost every individual who had any democratic thoughts at all was sending good wishes to the *Daily Worker*. Even Gracie Fields sent us a good luck message. "Reit good luck to t' *Daily Worker*—reit good luck, laad. Tell 'em I'll be reit glad when there's more work i' Lancashire," she told one of our reporters in May.

No one can question that, within the limits of its technical resources, a really first-class *Daily Worker* was being produced in 1939. The paper was extremely alert, responded quickly to the rapidly changing events and gave a fighting lead. The "Worker's Notebook," now signed by Walter Holmes, was firmly established as a popular favourite. In the Labour movement itself there was a great deal of activity, especially in the fight against unemployment and Fascism. This was strongly reflected in the columns of the paper.

The unemployed had signalised the New Year by appearing in the West End with a coffin on which was inscribed: "He did not get winter relief." Dense crowds applauded this demonstration but the police made various attempts to capture the coffin. They were unsuccessful. A couple of days later the coffin turned up at Downing Street, this time bearing the words: "Unemployed—No Appeasement." There was the usual tussle with the police.

On January 8, there took place that great, unforgettable demonstration at the Empress Hall, London, to welcome back the members of the International Brigade and to pay tribute to the 543 Britons who had made the supreme sacrifice in the fight against Fascism in Spain. No one who was present will ever forget the solemnity of the occasion.

The *Daily Worker* also published during January the stirring manifesto of the Communist Party announcing its "Crusade for the Defence of the British People." Keynote of the manifesto was the slogan, "Chamberlain Must Go!" and a call for Labour unity in order to establish a government "pledged to democracy and social advance, the defence of the people, and the carrying out of a real policy of peace."

In February Sir Stafford Cripps launched his People's Petition which represented a popular movement against the war danger and in defence of living standards. It evoked a wide response. For this action he was promptly expelled from the Labour Party despite the fact that at his Scottish rallies he had recruited 3,000 new members for his party. His expulsion was followed by that of Aneurin Bevan and G.R. Strauss. But all over the country great rallies were held which proved that Cripps had touched a popular chord. Since then, of course, all three Petitioners have made their peace with Transport House, have become Ministers of the Crown and turned on their comrades of the Popular Front days.

The mass movement in Britain was awakening, though it was not strong enough to hold up the plans of the warmongers. The principal responsibility for this situation rested on the shoulders of the right wing leaders of the Labour Party. By the expulsion of Cripps and his supporters they sought to frighten the left and raised the bogey of a split in the movement. By supporting the policy of the imperialists at every decisive movement they confused the workers and prevented effective action from being taken. This we have clearly seen in the case of Spain and Munich. After the imperialist policy had been carried through then out would come the Labour leaders with rolling phrases of criticism which served to rehabilitate them in the Labour movement but which represented for all practical purposes so many words and nothing more.

In February, too, came the fatal recognition of Franco by the Chamberlain Government against which the Labour Party vigorously protested at a Trafalgar Square demonstration. But what was the value of this protest when by their whole policy of supporting non-intervention and of leaving Spain in the lurch the Labour leaders had made a signal contribution to the Fascist victory over the Republican forces?

At that same demonstration, faced with vigorous cries from the crowd for Cripps, Herbert Morrison had retorted in vicious anger that "the Communist Party are agents of Franco." And this to a crowd that included many members of the Communist Party who had fought in the ranks of the International Brigade! Morrison was giving an assurance to Chamberlain that despite criticisms of his pro-Fascist policy the Labour leaders regarded the Communists as the major enemy.

Commenting on the recognition of Franco, the *Daily Worker* wrote: "Once again, as at Munich, three consequences are plainly visible to all. First, a direct aid to the Fascist enemy. Secondly, a direct weakening of the defences of the British and French people. Thirdly, as a result of the first two, an immediate and terrible increase in the international war danger." In the House of Commons the voice of Gallacher rang out again. "You ought to be impeached as a traitor to Britain," he shouted to Chamberlain when he made his statement.

Looking back and tracing the pattern of events, it is simple to see the plan of the Nazis' conspiracy against world peace and how they were systematically encouraged by the British and French Governments. This time the Nazis struck at Czechoslovakia in order to complete the job which had been begun at Munich. On March 15, Hitler occupied Czechoslovakia without meeting with resistance and proclaimed the Republic a German Protectorate. The occupation of Memel followed a week later. Madrid fell the following week, after two-and-a-half years of glorious resistance. On Good Friday, April 7, Mussolini seized Albania.

These events gave added weight to the *Daily Worker* editorial comment of March 16: "Unless there is organised swiftly a world peace front, pulling together the overwhelming power of the peaceful nations, the peoples of Britain and France face a threat of 'surrender or war' as grave as any Czechoslovakia faced."

Chamberlain was now compelled to face the results of his own policy so he struck up a somewhat fighting attitude, foreshadowed the introduction of conscription and talked about making a pact with Poland. But his basic policy of egging on Nazi Germany against the Soviet Union did not change and he continued to reject the Soviet proposals for the maintenance of peace. Thus the Soviet proposal on March 21 for a Six Power Conference was not taken up. In a private letter, quoted by his biographer, Chamberlain wrote on March 26: "I must confess to the most profound distrust of Russia. I have no belief in her ability to maintain an effective offensive, even if she wanted to. And I distrust her motives, which seem to me to have little connection with our ideas of liberty, and to be concerned only with getting everyone else by the ears. Moreover, she is both hated and suspected by many of the smaller States, notably by Poland, Rumania and Finland." This was the authentic voice of Blimp speaking. The *Daily Worker* had the full measure of this man and did not hesitate to step up its campaign for his removal from office as the only guarantee of peace.

A few days before the Nazi occupation of Czechoslovakia, Stalin had delivered a speech at the 18th Congress of the Communist Party of the Soviet Union which contained a profound analysis of the international situation and an exposition of the policy of the Soviet Government. It received very little attention in the British Press which then had 20-24 pages a day. The *Daily Worker* drew attention to the fact that the newspapers which gave great headlines to every statement by the aggressors had virtually boycotted this vitally important statement by Stalin. It is a point to be remembered in these days when the Press lords are campaigning for more paper on the grounds that they have insufficient space to keep the public informed about home and foreign affairs. Clearly, most of the editors shared Chamberlain's view of the Soviet Union. To them she did not count militarily. But if the British public had been fully informed about the contents of this speech and had studied it carefully the course of world events might have been altered.

Stalin's speech was, in part, addressed to Chamberlain for he pointed out that "the big and dangerous political game which the adherents of the policy of non-intervention have started, may end in serious fiasco for themselves." Dunkirk took place one year later. He emphasised that the Press of Britain, France and the U.S. were raising such a fuss as if they wanted to provoke a conflict between Germany and the Soviet Union. "If there are such madmen in Germany it is certain that we shall find a sufficient quantity of strait-jackets for them." The strait-jackets were found all right, thereby disproving Chamberlain's theory about the military weakness of Russia.

Stalin also warned that the Soviet Union could not be used to pick the chestnuts out of the fire for others, that the Soviet

Union stood four square against aggressive policies and that it intended to strengthen the fighting power of the Red Army and the Red Navy to the utmost.

But Chamberlain continued on his headlong course while at the same time pretending, in order to keep the public calm, that the Government was acting in consultation with the Soviet Union. In fact, he was still actively collaborating with the Nazis; he had sent a delegation of the Federation of British Industries to Dusseldorf to negotiate a trade deal with the German industrialists, he raised no objection to the German trade deal forced on Rumania which brought that country's resources under Nazi control, and he continued to dither on the question of a guarantee to Poland despite the growing Nazi threat to Danzig.

On March 30 the *Daily Worker* caused a great political sensation when it published the call of the Communist Party for the formation of a new Government headed by Attlee, Sinclair and Churchill. "Every day's delay in removing Chamberlain is dangerous and criminal," said the appeal. "The house is burning, and the Fire Brigades are in league with the fire-raisers who are only interested in drawing the insurance—which for them means the establishment of Fascism in Britain."

The appeal fell on deaf ears. For Attlee was as much afraid of Communism as Chamberlain himself and Churchill was speculating on the possibility of joining Chamberlain in the Government. In his memoirs he has written: "I should certainly have joined the Government had I been invited." Moreover, the mass of the people were confused by the course of events and the anti-Soviet barrage in the Press prevented them from realising that the Soviet Union was a strong and reliable ally with whom we could have formed an effective alliance for the defeat of Fascism. That understanding was not to come until 1941 and a heavy price had to paid for the delay.

When on that Good Friday, April 7, Mussolini invaded little Albania, the *Daily Worker* was immediately on the streets with the news. On that day there were no newspapers, but by the evening the Saturday number of the *Daily Worker* was being sold far and wide in London and as a result of the splendid rally by our supporters no less than 20,000 copies were disposed of. It was a remarkable achievement.

There now began that extremely tortuous period in the history of British diplomacy when the course of world events compelled Chamberlain to enter into negotiations with the Soviet Union although he maintained to the last his basic policy of provoking a conflict between Germany and the Soviet Union in the hope that out of such a war he would be able to weaken Communism and gain pickings for the benefit of British imperialism. He pursued this policy in spite of Stalin's warning that he would not be provoked into such a war and that Russia would not pick the chestnuts out of the fire for another Power.

British guarantees had already been given to both Poland and Rumania but they were obviously of no military value unless a general agreement was also secured with the Soviet Union. On April 16 the Soviet Government made a dramatic attempt to reach agreement with Britain and France and laid before them

WILLIAM RUST

(1903-1949)

first editor of the *Daily Worker*,
at his desk in Farringdon Road

Our first editorial and business offices,
41 Tabernacle Street, E.C.2

*Workers of the World Unite!*

# DAILY WORKER

No. 1     **WEDNESDAY, JANUARY 1, 1930**     One Penny

# WOOLLEN WORKERS TAKE THE FIELD

## REVOLUTION IN INDIA GROWS

### Congress Chiefs Feel Mass Pressure

The All-India National Congress, which opened at Lahore yesterday, adopted by 943 votes, against 799, the resolution moved by Gandhi, deploring the throwing of a bomb at the Viceroy and congratulating him on his escape. The minority, waving Red Flags, raised angry protests. Ghandhi's second motion is to deal with the new manœuvre of withdrawal of "Dominion status" in favour of independence.

The reports of meetings of the Congress Committee in Session since Christmas Day, shows that the enormous rising tide of the Indian masses, led by the fierce Indian proletariat whose determined fight, marked by mass political action, is the enormous motive force which has compelled the leaders of the Indian bourgeosie, who have in the past two years gone over to the side of British Imperialism, to make a desperate attempt to retain their hold on the masses by a show of opposition.

The resolution of the bourgeois nationalist leaders in favour of independence and boycott of legislature significantly leaves the campaign for civil disobedience and non-payment of taxes to the discretion of the Congress Committee, "as and when necessary."

At the Sikh Conference meeting yesterday, also in Lahore, Kharak Singh, the president, stated that out of thirty-one recent death sentences on revolutionary Indian nationalists, twenty-seven were Sikhs.

When Sir Frederick Sykes, Governor of Bengal, visited Ahmedabad two days ago he was met by a demonstration outside the station waving flags and with shouts of "Frederick Sykes, go back."

## SIXTY DEATHS IN CINEMA FIRE

### Many Children Amongst The Victims

A fire which broke out at the Glen Cinema, Paisley, near Glasgow, during a children's matinée yesterday afternoon, caused a panic, resulting, it is feared, in about sixty deaths.

As soon as news of the fire spread frantic mothers ran to the Cinema, and began searching for their children.

One hundred and fifty people were taken to hospital.

It is certain that at least six children are dead.

### FASCISTS WOUND WORKERS

Hanover, Tuesday.—On Sunday night sixteen armed Fascists attacked a group of workers who were leaving a Party local in a thoroughly working-class quarter.

The Fascists fired on the unarmed workers and wounded four of them seriously. As usual, the police arrived too late.—*Imprecor.*

## PRINCE'S JAUNT

### To Travel Into Impenetrable Jungle—By Train

### WITH HIS VALET!

On Friday the Prince of Wales will again start a jaunt that will cost thousands of pounds of the money the workers have earned for him.

He is going to Capetown, and from there will journey into the jungle—by train!

There he will display his intrepidity against the wild beasts of Africa. His valet is to accompany him, probably to hold the rifle.

An official of the "Kenilworth Castle," on which he is to travel, states that he is expected to play a prominent part in the "strenuous" deck games which are to be played on board.

"Otherwise, he will use an ordinary first-class cabin with the usual dressing-room."

### SHOOTING THE UNEMPLOYED

#### Social Democrat Police Chief Orders Massacre in Cologne

Berlin, Tuesday.—Yesterday evening 10,000 unemployed workers demonstrated in front of the Cologne Town Hall in order to support the proposal of the Communist faction for winter assistance for the unemployed.

The social democratic Police President was in charge of large forces of police, who tried to prevent the demonstrators from reaching the Town Hall. At first the police used their batons, but when their efforts proved ineffective the Social Democrat gave the order to fire.

Many workers were wounded by the police bullets and over 100 arrested, including the Communist, W. Deputy Kolwen. The Communist proposals in the Town Council were rejected.—*Imprecor.*

### CLOSING THE RANKS

#### Woollen Workers Consolidate Against Wage Cuts

*From Our Own Correspondent.*

Shipley, Tuesday.—Rank and file conferences are to be called in the textile area to consolidate the workers' resistance to the threatened wage cuts.

To counter the proposed woollen wages' enquiry, the Bradford district committee of the Communist Party issued to-day a statement to all wool workers.

The statement compares the statement with the Lancashire arbitration, which served the same purpose of breaking the workers' resistance.

The woollen textile workers are advised not to return to work, but to extend the struggle, and to build up mill committees of action to fight against the strike-breaking court of enquiry proposed by the Labour Government.

## MASS STRIKES AGAINST WAGE REDUCTIONS

### Police Attack Pickets

## ALL WORKERS SOLID AND DETERMINED TO WIN FIGHT

OVER two thousand woollen textile workers are on strike. The attempt to cut wages is meeting with real mass resistance. The workers are in a militant mood and maintain the utmost solidarity against employers, Labour Government, trade union bureaucrats and police.

The young workers are especially active and are giving increasing support to the Communist Party Campaign for rank and file Committees of Action.

### BONDFIELD, SCAB;

#### Labour Prepares to Smash Wool Strike

*(From Our Own Correspondent.)*

Bradford.—The council of the wool textile employers has not yet convened on the letter of the Minister of Labour proposing to set up a court of enquiry into the situation in the woollen industry under Part 2 of the Industrial Courts Act, 1919.

Before availing themselves of the offer to impose the wage reductions by means of arbitration the woollen bosses are anxiously watching the strikes which are repeatedly breaking out and being carried on with remarkable determination.

I understand that Margaret Bondfield is going ahead with the setting up of the Court and that the constitution and terms of reference will be announced shortly.

### DYE WORKERS STRIKE

#### Lightning Strike follows Dismissals

There was a lightning strike of 200 dye workers at the Kirk Lane Dye Works on Monday. The strike was due to the dismissal on the Saturday of 100 men.

Pickets were placed on the gates in the early morning and only the office staff and the key men on the mechanical side remained at work.

So far there is no news of a settlement and the works remain closed.

### VOTE AGAINST WAGE CUTS

The strike at the Prospect Mills, Padsey, continues. In answer to the opening of the mills in an attempt to impose a reduction of 1s. 6d. in the pound, a well-attended meeting of strikers held at the Trades Hall decided unanimously to resist any cut in wages. A new section of the workers. A strike committee was elected and pickets appointed.

All operatives, union and non-union, are out.

### DEFIANT SPIRIT

#### Determined to Resist Lower Wages

*(From Our Own Correspondent.)*

Saddleworth.—The attempt of the Saddleworth millowners to break the strike in nine mills against a wage cut of two shillings in the pound has completely failed. Although the mills were opened on Monday morning, only one of the thirteen hundred strikers, mostly women and girls, returned.

The police have repeatedly attacked the pickets and some arrests have been made. The defiant attitude of Lily Hutton, a young woman worker, when "on trial" for assaulting a burly police inspector, typifies the spirit of the workers.

A long period of short time and low wages has made them determined to resist to the utmost.

Tom Thurlbeck, who was fined £10 or two months on a charge of assaulting the police at the mill gates, has now been released, the workers having collected sufficient money to pay his fine.

### GREENFIELD STRIKE

#### Employers appeal to Labour Govt.

The operatives of the Kinders Mill, Greenfield, Yorks, are on strike and pickets are operating at the mills.

The employers' secretary has sent the following telegram to the Home Secretary:—

"Operatives of Messrs. Buckley and Co. (Greenfield), Ltd., Kinders Mill, Greenfield, Yorkshire, are being prevented by pickets from entering the mill, and are being otherwise intimidated at their homes. I am to ask that you will take such steps as will obviate intimidation of the workers and afford them adequate protection."

SCOTTISH D.P.C. "DAILY WORKER" PRIZE DRAW. 1st: 15556; 2nd: 7036; 3rd: 5569; 4th: 7004; 5th: 15466; 6th: 3776.

*The very first Daily Worker*

Cayton Street, City Road, our second home—
before the bomb fell, and after

# Daily Worker

No. 3438    REGISTERED AT THE G.P.O. AS A NEWSPAPER    One Penny

TUESDAY, JANUARY 21, 1941    ★ ★ ★ ★

# WORKERS MOBILISE AGAINST GOVERNMENT'S THREATS

### BY FRANK PITCAIRN

THE GREAT COUNTER-ATTACK OF THE MEN ON THE JOB AGAINST THE MEN ON THE MONEY-BAGS IS PUSHING FORWARD IN THIS COUNTRY ON ALL FRONTS.

With " conscription of labour " due for discussion at the next meeting of the Commons—date of it cannot be mentioned under present Government regulations—with a Rushka going on from the Government, the official Labour leaders and the capitalist Press against the People's Convention, which stands for defence of trade union rights and wage rights, stands for better pay and conditions in the Army,

workers in and out of uniform are rallying to the defence of themselves, their standards, their pay, their rights.

#### Defend Communist Party

And they rallied, too, in defence of the Communist Party and its Press—recognised as playing a leading part in the fight for better things, and for this reason threatened by the rich men's Government.

In South Wales, soldiers in uniform travelled from villages miles away to Llanelli and Swansea to hear William Gallacher, M.P. for West Fife, denounce the policy of the Tory-Labour coalition Government, and explain the progressive policy of the Communist Party.

Three thousand workers were at those meetings—held immediately after Swansea's worst air raid of the war. They made it very clear that when the rich attack the aims of the Communist Party they are attacking also the aims of the South Wales miners, platers, and factory workers.

Military police were mobilised and posted by the Government to prevent the soldiers attending these meetings.

This itself was a significant admission of the real feeling in the Army and the real fears of the Brasshats.

Two thousand soldiers in a single camp heard, by means of great ingenuity on the part of all concerned, the message of the People's Convention as brought to them by their delegate, and with one accord denounced the

(Continued on Page 8, Column 3)

#### STRIKES: THE REAL FACTS

Communists have been accused of fomenting strikes by the yellow Press.

Strikes which took place in 1940 included :

Seven strikes of miners to prevent reduction of pay. One stay-down strike to get a victimised workmen's inspector reinstated.

Two strikes of mill workers against the introduction of more looms.

One rail strike to prevent deduction of pay for time lost travelling.

Five strikes of building workers for increased pay and against victimisation.

One strike of steel workers for pay at recognising rates and 300 shipyard workers locked out for demanding tool allowance.

Who foments the strikes the Communists or the employers?

## BRITISH NOW IN ERITREA

BRITISH mobile forces were reported yesterday to be invading the Italian tied Sea colony of Eritrea.

This news followed the recapture of Kassala, the border town in the Anglo-Egyptian Sudan. It is understood that the British are now some miles inside Italian territory.

Meanwhile, General Wavell is preparing to deliver a blow for the capture of the Italian Mediterranean base of Tobruk.

British bombers hammered the town for two nights in succession on the second visit they caused a huge fire near a number of petrol dumps.

A spokesman of the Greek Ministry in Athens said on Sunday night that in spite of bad weather conditions Greek forces had advanced their lines.

An Italian communique stated there is " melting of importance to report on the Greek front." The same communique stated that the British raided Tobruk. "One plane was shot down it said, and goes on:

"On the Sudan front an Italian post repelled a strong enemy attack and prisoners were made. Our planes bombed British defences and troops at various points. Enemy air force carried out several raids on Eritrean territory."

## First Men For Fire Watch

THE first men to be called under the new Government fire-watching Order will be those 30's and the over 60's. The Order, which came into force yesterday, calls for 48 hours service per month and will apply to all except those who claim exemption on grounds of hardship or physical infirmity.

Every occupier of premises to which the Order applies must, within 14 days, notify in writing to the appropriate authority the arrangements made by him, and it will be his duty to carry out the arrangements as approved by the authority.

(See other story on Page Seven)

## DEATH OF DAME LLOYD GEORGE

The death of Dame Margaret Lloyd George, wife of Mr. David Lloyd George, was announced yesterday.

She was unable to be with her husband at Churt on Mr. Lloyd George's 78th birthday last Friday because she was confined to bed.

Married in 1888, Dame Margaret was the daughter of Mr. Richard Owen, of Cricieth, celebrated her golden wedding three years ago.

## MUST HAVE INCREASE, SAY RAILWAYMEN

From Our Own Correspondent

A CROWDED meeting at the Manchester and District Council of the National Union of Railwaymen on Sunday passed a resolution insisting that their National Executive Committee take action to press their claim for a 10s. wage increase.

The meeting was attended by 90 delegates representing 80 branches and 25,000 men.

Vigorously supporting the resolution, A Rilyard poured scorn on the idea that because there was a war railwaymen should tamely accept promises of something sometime in the war is over.

" We must see that the terms upon which the Labour Party entered the Government are carried into effect," he said, " and we demand some of those promised doses of Socialism now, not something indefinite in the dim, distant future "

J. H. Potts, the president, said that workers everywhere were going short of the things that make life worth-while, but on the other hand it was noticeable that the monied classes could still enjoy their pre-war standard of life.

We must get something more than wages we must get control of the industry in which we work, he added

The resolution passed at the meeting reads:

" That this mass meeting of represe

sentatives and officials of the N.U.R. area representing 25,000 railwaymen in South Lancashire and Cheshire, view with alarm the sharp rise in the cost of living which, together with the added difficulties of the present time, place thousands of railwaymen on a lower standard of life than is desirable, or compatible with today's needs

" We therefore instruct the Executive Committees of the N.U.R. to spare no effort in taking representatives to the railway companies and to the Government to grant any demands for an increase of 10s. per week for all railwaymen. In addition, no contracted delays should be tolerated in pressing the Railways Executive Committee for an immediate reply to our demand."

The last number before the ban

Any communication on the
subject of this letter should be
addressed to :—
THE UNDER SECRETARY OF STATE,
HOME OFFICE,
LONDON S.W.1.
and the following number quoted :—
865,003/117.

HOME OFFICE,
WHITEHALL.

26th August, 1942.

Gentlemen,

I am directed by the Secretary of State to inform you
that he has this day revoked the Order made by him on the
17th January, 1941, under Regulation 2D of the Defence
(General) Regulations, 1939, applying the provisions of that
Regulation to the newspaper known as the "Daily Worker".

The Secretary of State has also revoked the Orders made
by him on the 17th January, 1941, under Regulation 94B of
the said Regulations directing that none of the printing
presses in England or in Scotland under the control of the
Kestle (Press) Limited shall be used until the leave of the
High Court in England or of the High Court of Justiciary in
Scotland, as the case may be, has been obtained.

I am to point out that the decision to revoke the Order
made in January 1941 under Defence Regulation 2D derogates in
no way from the power and duty of the Secretary of State to
make a fresh Order under this Regulation if at any future
date there should be systematic publication of matter
calculated to foment opposition to the prosecution of the war
to a successful issue.

I am,
Gentlemen,
Your obedient Servant,

Ja Newsam

The Editorial Board of
the "Daily Worker",
Premier House,
150, Southampton Row, W.C.1.

Mr. Morrison revokes …

The ban is lifted—William Rust inspecting the first copy
off the press, September 6, 1942

ONE PENNY

**PASS THIS ON TO A FRIEND—**

# Daily Worker

LATE EDITION

**—TEN READERS FOR EVERY COPY!**

No. 3431    MONDAY, SEPTEMBER 7, 1942

## STALINGRAD BEATS OFF ANOTHER MASS GERMAN ASSAULT

### *Von Bock's South-West Drive Fails*

**V**ON BOCK'S SECOND AND GREATEST MASS ONSLAUGHT AGAINST THE HEROIC CITY OF STALINGRAD HAS BEEN SMASHED AND THE RESISTANCE OF THE DEFENDERS IS STIFFENING, ACCORDING TO A DESPATCH FROM MOSCOW LATE LAST NIGHT.

Though the situation must remain grave while 50 German divisions with thousands of tanks and planes are continuously battering at the gates of the city, the drive from the south-west has failed, cables Reuter's special correspondent, that was confirmed by the Moscow communique yesterday:—

"All German attempts to break through to the city are meeting with staunch resistance from Soviet troops," it was reported. "During the past 24 hours the Germans have made four attempts to attack one fortified sector, all of which were unsuccessful."

### Malta Gunners Greet Us

CABLE AND WIRELESS

*Via Imperial*

### Harry Pollitt's Appeal

I APPEAL, on behalf of the Central Committee of the Communist Party, to every member and every organisation to raise all the energies in the way we all work for the victory of the Daily Worker.

*This Daily Worker is our fighting tool. We are all going to prove we know how to use it. Now to apply it in every job we are on. It is a tool that every worker, skilled and unskilled, man or woman, can use.*

It can be used by every man and woman, because it is the people's paper, fighting a people's fight for a people's victory and a people's peace

#### From JOHN GIBBONS
*Daily Worker Special Correspondent*

MOSCOW, Sunday night.

**T**HE great Stalingrad battle rages with undiminishing intensity. With first grey masks of dawn German Junkers and Messerschmitts come over in their hundreds trying by bombing and machine-gunning to pulverise Soviet defences.

### How to Win the War

### *DAILY WORKER'S POLICY*

*The following declaration of the aims of the Daily Worker has been adopted by the Editorial Board*

**O**N this historic day of re-publication the Daily Worker thanks all those of the Labour, trade union, co-operative and democratic movements whose magnificent support has succeeded in removing the nineteen months' ban, but also very considerably strengthened the unity of the people in the fight for victory over Fascism.

The Daily Worker, as our fighting tool, belongs to you who make it, rebirth possible, solemnly pledges to repay all you have done by the service it will give in the struggle to destroy the Hitlerite enemy.

We shall speak for Britain, for a wide national unity, firmly buttressed by a united working class.

We shall speak for the millions of ordinary folk, the men and women in industry and the services, whose toil and courage and sacrifice will bring victory and the new world of security.

The people want the truth: we shall give it to them—

### £50,000

63,336 196, 7s. in last days!

This is the second sum onto our Fighting Fund since the lifting of the ban.

### Drive Rommel Back From Our Minefields

RUSSELL'S Attack Clogs has now been posted back onto of our minefield on the Egypt battlefront through which they advanced a score ago

#### WILLIE'S TOUR
Mr. Wardart Welfoin, after leaving the Egyptians from yesterday said:—

"My impression is that what has taken place here today and the retreating days has renewed the desert thrust by Egypt.

"The battlefield I have seen the desert is an object lesson to the normally the more essential.

---

Our third home (1942-1948),
74 Swinton Street, Gray's Inn Road

The Daily Worker co-operative society's first annual meeting, Memorial Hall, Farringdon Street (1946) with—inset—voting for the management committee

The banner reads: PEOPLE'S PRESS *Support the* PRESS

*For* CO-OPERATION

A great anniversary meeting: the Albert Hall, January, 1948

# Daily Worker

MONDAY NOVEMBER 1 1948

# TORCHLIGHT WELCOME TO THE NEW PAPER

## Twenty thousand cheer as the first copies roll off the press

From SAM RUSSELL and PETER FRYER

## FRENCH STRIKE SOLID AFTER FIVE WEEKS

### Tanks fail to raise coal

## A reminder —we still need cash

### £832

### West still claims 'no agreement'

### PO Engineers put case for more pay today

### Inquiry on 'bribes' to open today

### Zenith of years, says Pollitt

### A HUGE DEMAND

### BERNARD SHAW

### A FLOOD OF SHARES

### MUKDEN STREET FIGHTING

The first number of the new paper produced at Farringdon Road

William Rust House, 75 Farringdon Road, E.C.I

1930: editorial office, Tabernacle Street

1949: editorial office, Farringdon Road

Chairing the Editor, Farringdon Road, October 31, 1948

William Rust holds up the first copy to the giant crowd demonstrating in Clerkenwell Green and Farringdon Road, October 31, 1948

proposals for the establishment of a united front of mutual assistance. If these proposals had been accepted the world war could have been averted. But Chamberlain kept these proposals secret and delayed his answer. Only the *Daily Worker* maintained a consistent campaign for an alliance with the Soviet Union. On April 18 it reproved Herbert Morrison for an article in the *Forward* in which he had stated that "the Soviet Union should make clear to the world where she stands and not engage in too much official 'public silence.'" The *Daily Worker* answered that "if there is one country which has made its position clear that country is the Soviet Union.… The duty of Herbert Morrison and the millions of British people who passionately desire peace, is to force the British Government to accept the proposals of the Soviet Union."

Twenty-one days were to pass before Chamberlain deigned to answer the Soviet proposals of April 16. On May 7 he sent a Note to Moscow rejecting the offer. Chamberlain proposed instead that the Soviet Government should oblige itself to render immediate assistance to Great Britain and France in the event of their being involved in war under their guarantees to Poland and Rumania. But he gave no guarantee of assistance to the Soviet Union on the part of Britain and France should the Soviet Union become involved in war as a result of its obligations towards States in Eastern Europe.

Even before this reply was received it was evident to the Soviet Government that the Western Powers did not mean business. The war situation was becoming extremely serious and it was therefore decided to put the direction of foreign policy into stronger hands. On May 3 it was announced that Molotov, the Prime Minister, had replaced Litvinov as Foreign Secretary and that he would retain the Premiership.

On May 31, Molotov clearly summed up the issues at stake and declared that the creation of an effective peace front required the following minimum conditions:

"The conclusion between Great Britain, France and the U.S.S.R. of an effective pact of mutual assistance against aggression, of an exclusively defensive character; a guarantee of the States of Central and Eastern Europe, including without exception all the European countries bordering on the U.S.S.R. against an attack by aggressors; the conclusion of a definite agreement on the forms and extent of the immediate and effective assistance to be rendered to one another and to the guaranteed States in the event of an attack by aggressors."

Molotov also pointedly questioned the sincerity of the British attitude. "At present one cannot even say whether there is really a serious desire to give up the 'non-intervention' policy." The *Daily Worker* was the only paper to publish his speech in full.

Meanwhile, in Britain the peace campaign of the Communist Party and the *Daily Worker* was gathering wide support, the Conservative critics of the Government, led by Churchill, were becoming more critical and Lloyd George had entered the lists against the warmongers. Moreover, the signing of the "Pact of Steel" between Ribbentrop and Ciano on May 22 had destroyed the hopes of some British politicians that they would be able to separate Italy from Germany. Chamberlain was compelled to manoeuvre.

The Foreign Office handed out the story that the principle of reciprocity in mutual aid had been agreed upon but there were differences over the Baltic States of Estonia, Latvia and Finland which did not want to be guaranteed by the Soviet Government. And Chamberlain, who had philosophically resigned himself to the destruction of the sovereign rights of the Governments of Spain, Austria and Czechoslovakia, now found himself unable to bring pressure on the Baltic States. To resolve these differences Chamberlain announced on June 7 the sending to Moscow of a Foreign Office clerk, a certain Mr. Strang. Eden had volunteered to go but the offer was rejected by Chamberlain. Since those days Mr. Strang has advanced somewhat further in his career. He is now Sir William and the permanent head of the Foreign Office.

Under the heading "Office Boy Goes on Tramp," the *Daily Worker* asked "why the negotiations could not have been concluded immediately in London and why, if it was necessary to send an envoy at all, it was not a member of the Government but a Foreign Office clerk?"

The negotiations went on all through July but the results were negligible. Finally, they were switched on to a military basis and the Government sent a military mission in August. Meanwhile, the *Daily Worker* kept up a constant agitation for the conclusion of the Pact as the sole means to prevent the outbreak of the world war. It was a lone voice. The military mission was headed by an obscure Admiral by the name of Sir Reginald Plunkett Ernle-Erle-Drax, and as though wishing to emphasise their leisurely approach to their tasks they travelled to Moscow by the sea route. It was later admitted that the mission had been sent without powers to make decisions. Negotiations collapsed over the right of the Red Army to enter Poland in fulfilment of its pledges under the proposed pact of mutual assistance. The farce was ended.

On the evening of Tuesday, August 22, there was a big rush in the streets of London to buy copies of the next day's *Daily Worker* which reported the news that a non-aggression pact was about to be signed between Germany and the Soviet Union and which contained a statement by the Central Committee of the Communist Party on this momentous event. Over twenty thousand extra copies were sold. Newsagents the next morning reported that they were sold out. The question was heard everywhere: "What does the *Daily Worker* say about it?"

The lessons drawn by the Communist Party were very simple. It stated that "Hitler is forced to recognise the strength and power of the Soviet Union and his dreams of crushing it have received a setback." It demanded an ending of the double-dealing policy which had turned the negotiations on the Anglo-Soviet Pact into a shameful farce, it called for the immediate conclusion of the Pact and said "Let Chamberlain and Daladier fly to Moscow and open up direct conversations with the Soviet Government." But it had to be recognised that Hitler was the master of the world situation at that moment. He was determined to wage war without delay and, in view of the refusal of the Western Powers to come to terms with the Soviet Union and in the face of the obvious weakness of the Western Powers and influential position of the Fifth Column, he decided to strike first in the West.

In this situation the soundest possible course for the Soviet Union was to avoid walking into the Chamberlain trap from the other end. If the Soviet Union, after the refusal of Chamberlain to sign a mutual assistance pact, had then refused to sign a non-aggression pact with Hitler, it is possible that the Nazis would have attacked the Soviet Union with the tacit support of the Western Powers. As it turned out the Soviet Government gained nearly two valuable years for the continuance of its defence preparations, it extracted important territorial concessions from the Nazis and tied up so many Nazi forces in the East that the invasion of Britain had to be abandoned.

G.D.H. Cole, in his *History of the Labour Party from 1914,* says that the German-Soviet Pact bewildered the Communists. Far be it from me to claim that we never made mistakes or that we always immediately got our bearings when a sharp change occurred in the world situation. But I must say that the Communist Party and the *Daily Worker* fully understood the meaning of this Pact as without doubt Chamberlain also did.

Sir Stafford Cripps later told in a speech delivered early in 1942 that he had advised "the British Government in the preceding June that the agreement would be made by September 1

… Stalin tried, I think quite genuinely, early in 1939 to get agreement with France and Britain. When it failed he was not ready himself to take on the Germans. He signed the agreement with Germany, and immediately production went ahead on a full war basis for the time when the Russians knew they would have to fight the Germans."

This view is confirmed by the statement of von Schulenburg, the then German Ambassador in Moscow, who as late as August 4 telegraphed to Berlin that "my overall impression is that the Soviet Government is at present determined to sign with England and France if they fulfil all Soviet wishes." And the Soviet wishes, let it be remembered, were the conclusion of a cast iron pact of mutual assistance against the threatened Fascist attack. Yet despite the indications of a change in Hitler's tactics, Chamberlain refused to sign on the dotted line with Stalin. Possibly he hoped that Hitler would never make a *volte-face* or that if he did it would be only a temporary one. During the period of the phony war many British statesmen reproached Hitler for his abandonment of "Germany's traditional anti-Communist policy" (Lord Kemsley), and there was much hopeful talk about the possibility of switching the war.

It suited the purpose, nevertheless, of the leaders of the Labour and Conservative parties to put the blame for the war on to the shoulders of Stalin, to further the legend that Communism and Fascism are the two sides of the same medal and to coin the expression "Communazis." Such propaganda served to switch attention from the years of appeasement, the sabotage of the

Anglo-Soviet Pact and the prevention of the building of the united front against Fascism. But the die was now cast and there was no turning back. The Nazis invaded Poland on September 1. On September 3, Britain and France declared war on Germany. The second world war had begun. For the *Daily Worker* there were difficult days ahead.

There are a number of other events of the 1939 pre-war days which are worth recording. The debate on the Cripps expulsion by the Labour Party Conference on May 29 ended with a vote for the Executive of 2,100,000 to 402,000, but it was an altogether disappointing event as Cripps laid down no challenge, made no attempt to argue a political case, and merely confined himself to the technicalities of his expulsion. An excellent opportunity to stage a fight was thrown away. Perhaps Cripps was already tiring of the fight and seeking other solutions.

All through this year the *Daily Worker* had been persistently carrying on its campaign for bomb-proof shelters which had been pioneered by Professor Haldane, whose book on A.R.P. had caused a national sensation. But Government policy was against deep shelters on the grounds that such protection would lower morale, and when the war actually came the authorities refused even to open the Tube stations as shelters until compelled to give way to the Londoners who simply took them over.

On May 18 Professor Haldane also wrote for us an article on uranium, which may not have been given much attention then, but was a grave warning as to the way in which science was being pressed into the service of war and the first indication in the popular Press of those trends in scientific research which were to culminate in the dropping of the atom bombs at Hiroshima and Nagasaki in August, 1945.

Explaining current experiments on the splitting of the uranium nucleus, Haldane foresaw the possibility of power being available in such vast quantities as to cause a colossal economic crisis in capitalist countries, and then went on to say: "Fortunately, uranium bombs cannot be at once adapted for war, as the apparatus needed is very heavy and also very delicate, so it cannot at present be dropped from an aeroplane. But doubtless uranium will be used for killing in some way." As we now know, the use of uranium for killing was pressed far more rapidly ahead than its use for constructive purposes. The world still awaits the application of uranium to the production of power.

## Chapter Seven
# The War—and Suppression

O N THE VERY eve of war, in its full-length leading article of August 30, 1939, the paper made its fundamental political position crystal clear. Declaring that the "frozen inactivity of the leadership of Labour" was "disastrous," the leader noted that their attitude seemed to be "Leave it all to Chamberlain." It went on:

"But to leave it all to Chamberlain is to leave it to elements who have in the past opened the gates to Fascist aggression … who have just rejected the aid of the Soviet Union…. It is nonsensical to argue that 'in this grave crisis we cannot raise the question of replacing the Government.' On the contrary, in this crisis we have got in sheer self-defence to get a Government composed of those who in recent years have shown their ability to fight for peace and the maintenance of democracy. Only such a Government will be in a position to mobilise all the democratic and peace forces of the world for a last-minute effort. And if war should come, if the Fascist aggressors should seek to trample all Europe underfoot, only such a Government could inspire the British people to successfully resist this and to smash Fascism utterly. Only such a Government would be in a position to ensure that the rich sympathisers of Fascism did not betray British people."

Those words have a prophetic ring in the light of later history. Their forthright penetration to the political heart of the matter—in other words, their sound class approach—was never missing from the *Daily Worker's* handling of the war situation at all its varied stages.

Not for nothing was the phrase the "phony war" to be coined as the apt term for this period. There was nothing but quietness on the Western Front. In the East the German blitzkrieg overwhelmed the weak military machine of gentry-ridden Poland, but was stopped short on the borders of Western White Russia and the Western Ukraine, liberated by an equally powerful and rapid Red Army advance. The Munichite Tory Press redoubled its propaganda for an eventual Anglo-German rapprochement against the "common danger" of Bolshevism (the *Daily Mail* pinpointed this "common danger" in the horrid fact that as the Soviet armies advanced over the old Polish frontier the landlords were dispossessed and the peasants got the land). Liberal and Labour spokesmen tirelessly purveyed anti-Soviet venom.

Across the Channel the true character of the war at this stage was startlingly symbolised in the contrast between the total inactivity of the Maginot Line and what M. Sarraut, Minister of the Interior, called the "daily increasing intensity" of the "internal offensive" to "clear out Communism," which the French Munichites had begun on the eve of the war by suppressing *L'Humanité*. "The Government will continue the purge without mercy," Sarraut cried. "They are devoting all their vigilance to this task, and will continue it until France is swept clean of the campaign of defeatism." History has since had a few words to say about who were the real defeatists in France in 1939-40, has she not?

On the home front the cost of living skyrocketed (local surveys showed that the increase was often four times as much as that recorded by the official index), real wages sagged, profiteering was colossal, the State industrial, raw material and foodstuff controls that were set up were all placed in the hands of the big monopolists. The leaders of the T.U.C., entering into the fullest collaboration with the Government and the employers, might call this "war Socialism"; it was more accurately described by the noted economist, Sir Arthur Salter, as the "bastard Socialism of the vested interests." The political and industrial "truce" was disarming and demoralising the entire Labour movement. The Government's sweeping Emergency Powers made it an absolute dictatorship.

It was clearly an impossible situation that no radical opposition was being expressed to this war which was not what it seemed, which (on the Chamberlain-Daladier side) really aimed at making Europe safe for plutocracy. But there were shrill cries of rage and dismay from the hostile and/or the fainthearted when the *Daily Worker* of Saturday, October 7, boldly blazoned to the world a manifesto of the Communist Party giving a basic exposure of the character of the war ("This war is not a war for democracy against Fascism … The British and French ruling class are seeking to use the anti-Fascist sentiments of the people for their own imperialist aims … When they speak of the 'overthrow of Hitlerism' they mean the setting up of some other kind of reactionary Government which will be their servant and carry out their anti-Soviet aims"). Outlining the heavy blows already falling on the people at home, the manifesto listed a series of simple economic and political demands—including freedom for India and the Colonies—and called "for the formation of a new Government which will carry out these demands" and which "will carry on peace negotiations in the interests of the people and in co-operation with the Soviet Union … to lay the basis for a peace that will bind the warmongers of all countries and strengthen democracy everywhere."

No one will pretend that such sharp opposition to a generally accepted war is an easy or popular task, but the *Daily Worker* did not shrink from it. On the contrary, it went into action with every gun blazing, showing as the weeks and months passed how it had really mastered the difficult art of consistent, skilful and hard-hitting agitation, how powerfully it could swim against the stream. That last quality was certainly necessary when the Soviet-Finnish war, opening at the end of November, let loose a tidal wave of anti-Soviet hysteria exceeding even the intervention outbursts of twenty years before or the "cold war" cries of ten years later. The most abject display came from the Labour leaders, who rushed to join pro-Finn committees presided over by the leading British Franco-ite, Lord Phillimore, and whose printed propaganda touched the most unprecedented depths of distortion, omission, scurrility and quotation-faking.

Alone the *Daily Worker* stood steady, piercing the pungent poison cloud of lies with the blast of cold, hard facts. Alone the *Daily Worker* told the truth about Finnish "democracy"—the semi-Fascist police State of the old Baltic Baron and White terrorist, "Butcher" Mannerheim, the banker Ryti and the Social-Democrat millionaire Tanner (subsequently to be jailed by his own countrymen as an arch-collaborator with the Germans). Alone the *Daily Worker* debunked the wildly wishful wires of the British correspondents (which Mr. Frank Owen, now *Daily Mail* Editor, was later to denounce as "scat-writing," "ludicrous when it was not simply mendacious").

Our determined stand unquestionably rallied the sober elements in the Labour movement. When *Reynolds News* opened up on the anti-Soviet side, its postbag of protest (December 10, 1939) was a record-breaker. Mr D.N. Pritt, K.C., Labour M.P. for North Hammersmith, refused to toe his Party's anti-Soviet line and was expelled. And in a very short space of time our warnings of the real character of the war, of the aim of the ruling class to switch it against the U.S.S.R., were to be spectacularly justified. Not only was war material—including 450 aeroplanes, 960 guns, 5,000 machine-guns, tens of millions of rounds of ammunition—rushed to the Finns; a fully-equipped expeditionary force of 50,000 men was made ready by Britain and France, and was standing by at the end of February.

Mr. Hore-Belisha, ex-Minister of War, chose just that moment to let the cat out of the bag in a newspaper article proclaiming that this was the opportunity for an Allied force to strike at Leningrad (had not *The Times* written, many years before, "Finland is the key to Leningrad, and Leningrad is the key to Moscow"?). A *Daily Worker* leader (February 19, 1940), noting that this sinister provocation had been submitted for Government approval before printing, commented that one thing was now abundantly clear—"the real meaning of the Finnish hullabaloo is to create a new war front and to establish a base for the long-planned war against the Soviet Union."

But history was moving far too fast for the conspirators. The Red Army turned and breached the fabulous Mannerheim Line ("No army can break through such a line," General Sir Walter Kirke had sapiently assured the Finns as late as the summer of 1939). Finnish resistance collapsed. In the middle of March a peace treaty confounding the anti-Sovietists by its moderation was signed in Moscow. And two years later Mr. Bevin's own union journal, the Transport and General Workers' *Record,* was to write in its issue of March, 1942, these words absolutely justifying our lone stand of 1939-40:

> "The Soviet Union was never more lied about and the policy of her Government never more misunderstood than during her war with Finland.... The decision of the Soviet Union to invade Finland, after negotiations for certain strategic positions had broken down, has been justified by events.... She had very good reasons for fearing that

William Rust's spread on the *Daily Worker's* tenth anniversary

Finland would be used as a jumping-off ground for an attack on the Soviet Union.... She took steps to secure strategic positions which would obstruct the attack when it came—as come it did 15 months later."

The Finnish war was barely a month old when the *Daily Worker* celebrated its tenth birthday; and we did it with a justifiable flourish. The issue of Saturday, December 30, 1939, was in full seven-column format (the then standard national newspaper style) instead of the usual six columns, with eight pages against the normal Saturday six. It was a gala as well as a fighting issue,

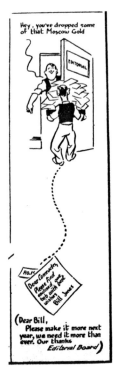

proudly presenting itself under the challenging headline: "Ten Years and Still Hitting Hard." A bold centre-spread by William Rust told the inspiring story of our first decade, concluding with these "four points for 1940": (1) a 50 per cent. increase in the Fighting Fund to £2,000 a month; (2) doubled circulation; (3) all-round improvement of news service, especially reports direct from factory and home; (4) building up of the *Daily Worker* Readers' Leagues so that they become "a steel framework round the paper." It was announced that George Allison was to take charge of the Leagues; and Violet Lansbury took over the Fund.

So we entered our eleventh year of life—that fateful year of 1940. Significantly enough the issue of January 1 splashed the news of a new attack on the paper. Sir Walter Citrine (as he then was) and six other members of the T.U.C. General Council had taken out a writ for libel against the *Daily Worker,* arising out of a series of articles on the situation in the French trade unions and the activities of the official Anglo-French Trade Union Council. When the case came on, at the end of April, we were brilliantly defended by Mr. D.N. Pritt, K.C., whose cross-examination of Citrine made it clear that the General Council leaders favoured the French industrial decrees which, by sapping militant trade unionism and demoralising the workers, were later to be described by Mr. Bevin himself as "one of the contributions to the French disaster."

OUR THANKS
TO THEM

THE SELLER
Brings your paper to you. More than that, he represents some of the hardest working and most faithful supporters of the paper; men and women like him stand for hours in rain and cold; rise while you are still in bed; meet trains at lonely provincial stations; form an indispensable part of the distribution machinery; help to defeat the wholesale newsagents' boycott of the Daily Worker; play a great part in the working-class movement. To them our very best thanks.

In the course of court proceedings Citrine incidentally admitted that a committee of union leaders and employers here had drafted a document containing a reference to the dangers of "excessive wages." Such admissions lent wide interest to the case, which ended with judgment for the plaintiffs. Their damages were not, however, sensational. Citrine was awarded £300, the total sum for the whole seven being £1,400. Mr. Justice Stable explained that he did not award damages which might put the *Daily Worker* out of action

(Above and opposite) more from the 10th anniversary edition

because "people were entitled to hold Communist views, express those views and criticise the views of others" and it was desirable that the *Daily Worker* should continue publication.

That judicial emphasis was valuable; for the T.U.C. leaders' action had encouraged the other enemies of the paper to open out. In February the Kemsley newspapers launched a waspish attack, which the cynical may well have thought not unrelated to the Noble Viscount's qualms over his pre-war overtures to Goebbels; though such instances of Big Business hostility could likewise not be dissociated from the lively campaign we opened in January under the slogan "Your Wages are in Peril." That campaign was pertinaciously pressed and contributed to the withdrawal of the late Lord Keynes' "deferred pay" scheme. And the readers gave the surest sign of their enthusiasm in the *Daily Worker's* cause by sending the Fund soaring over its new £2,000 target—with £21 to spare—in January, thereafter mounting steadily month by month to a record of £2,469 in April.

Enormous events were now at hand. As that freezing winter of 1940 gave way to spring the "phony war" cracked up. After a sudden lunge north, engulfing Denmark and Norway, the German blitzkrieg in May turned west in its fullest force. Holland and Belgium were overwhelmed in a matter of days and the Battle of France opened, with the B.E.F. hotly engaged on the critical northern sector. "Rearmament," however, had filled the pockets of the arms magnates and not the ammunition boxes of the inadequate British armour. Under-equipped, under-supplied, out-gunned and out-generalled by the enemy, Britain's gallant warriors were driven remorselessly back to the coast. The name "Dunkirk," compound of heroism and horror, was bloodily etched in our history and in the consciousness of the people.

The military and political crisis was of the greatest magnitude. The atmosphere was electric with confusion, alarm—and mounting popular anger. To defend the Tory rulers rather than the realm Home Secretary Sir John ("Bengal") Anderson* spun a

...................................................

* Former governor of Bengal who gave his name to the Anderson air-raid

new sinister web of Defence Regulations; among them were the newspaper-suppressing 2D and the imprisonment-without-trial 18B—to be used as much against foreign refugee anti-Fascists as against our native Mosleyites. The dirty slander was spread that the Communists were "fifth columnists"; hurling it back in the teeth of its perpetrators, Professor J.B.S. Haldane, on behalf of the *Daily Worker,* told a great Sheffield meeting that "in the five years during which he had been a reader of the paper, it was a provable fact that in nine cases out of ten the *Daily Worker* had been right, and had been the only newspaper that was right." Chamberlain was forced out of the Premiership but there was no decisive break with Chamberlainism. The arch-Municheer and his friends remained in the new coalition Cabinet headed by Churchill—promising "blood, toil, tears and sweat"—and including the Labour leaders. These last, commented William Rust (*Daily Worker,* May 20, 1940), "who sabotaged the People's Front that could have prevented war, who swore never to sully their 'Socialism' by co-operation in the cause of peace, are today in a war government alongside the worst Diehards."

No one can glance through the files of the *Daily Worker* for those tense Dunkirk days without a feeling of pride and confidence. As Chesterton once wrote of Bernard Shaw, "when the spirit who denies besieged the last citadel, blaspheming life itself, there was one especially whose voice was heard and whose spear was never broken." While panicky members of the upper class

........................................

shelter which failed to impress J.B.S. Haldane (see pp.166-7).—J.E.

and their intellectual hangers-on were fleeing over the Atlantic, the *Daily Worker* ranged over every current problem facing the people, informing, inspiring and guiding. Detailed and practical propositions were daily offered on the burning issues of evacuation and A.R.P. Attempts by employers and local gentry to give a class twist to the spontaneous Local Defence Volunteers (later the Home Guard) were countered with the demand for the maintenance of democracy in this body.

When Bevin and Morrison, howling "work like hell" and "go to it," threw the Factory Acts overboard, the *Daily Worker* (May 30) featured a solid scientific demonstration by Professor Haldane that the seven-day week would, in a few weeks, actually slow down munitions output. Six weeks later Mr. Bevin admitted that production was in fact on the decline and the Factory Act requirements would be reintroduced. A justified editorial "we-told-you-so" underscored the irony that "in the meantime the *Daily Worker* has been threatened by the Home Secretary for impeding the successful prosecution of the war!" (July 20).

All that the *Daily Worker* was hammering home—all our pin-pointing of the responsibility of the ruling class, the fatal error of silent and shut-eyed submission to Andersonite dictatorship, the need for the people to decide their own future—received shattering confirmation in the fall of France. "The collapse came from the top," wrote the Paris correspondent of *The Times;* and those words summed up everything. The French traitors had opened the front, above all when they "outlawed the great French Communist Party.... Nothing has contributed more to the Hitler victory than the destruction of democracy, this wilful crushing of the independence and initiative of the people" (leader, June 15, 1940). But "what of Britain? The same ruling class forces that brought disaster to France are still in control here" (June 18). The guilty must be brought to account, the lesson of France learnt, and—as the Communist Party proclaimed in its manifesto featured in our issue of Saturday, June 22—a "real People's Government" set up; "only then can the danger of Fascist invasion and tyranny be successfully withstood."

From now on the leadership of the movement for a People's Government became the central political campaign of the paper, thus consistently developing the line it had expounded even on the eve of the war, as the opening passages of this Chapter have shown. As that campaign grew and strengthened and drew in wider forces so the enemies of the *Daily Worker* stepped up their attacks. These are the two intertwined threads of our history during its next crucial stage.

Readers were made physically aware of the critical position of their paper when newsprint cuts forced us to appear, as from June 3, in a single instead of a double sheet—four half-size pages as against four full-size pages. But the miniature format at least compelled compression and economy in presentation and was retained (in the shape of eight half-size pages) when we contrived to resume our normal intake of newsprint on June 24. From the new tabloid front page readers learnt on June 8 of an important, indeed historic, step in the development and defence of the *Daily Worker*. This was the constitution of an Editorial

Board of outstanding personalities with Professor Haldane as chairman: the members were Sean O'Casey, famous dramatist; R. Page Arnot, noted Marxist writer and scholar; and Councillor Jack Owen, of Manchester, veteran militant engineer.

Within the next few days the new Editorial Board chairman had to issue a statement, headed "Those in High Places Fear Us," exposing the "systematic attempts" being made in many parts by the police and others, quite illegally, to intimidate *Daily Worker* sellers and newsagents. These moves were on a par with the trumping-up of cases against Communist speakers (Ben Bradley, hero of the Meerut Trial*, was jailed for three months in one of these affairs) and the use of 18B to hold without trial Johnny Mason, A.E.U. shop steward, on unspecified charges of "hampering war production."

Then, on July 10, a more serious threat was made. A letter from the Home Secretary threatened to suppress the paper under Regulation 2D, unless it ceased what was called its "systematic publication of matter calculated to foment opposition to the prosecution of the war." When Professor Haldane asked what items were complained of he received the shuffling answer that the Home Secretary "cannot attempt, by reference to particular items, to give you guidance" how to avoid suppression under 2D; the "general tenor" of the paper would determine whether action were taken. The purely arbitrary nature of the threat, and the powers behind it, was thus made perfectly clear. It led

......................................................

* See p.63.—J.E.

to the *Daily Worker* receiving full backing at a conference held under the auspices of the National Council for Civil Liberties on July 21; and wide support was won in the House of Commons for an amendment to remove the dictatorial powers of 2D—which, it was recalled, was an invasion-scare supplement to the initial Regulation 2C, empowering the suppression of newspapers, but only after due trial. The threat pushed the Fighting Fund up to the new record of £2,904.

Under the hammer-blows of defeat and national danger, the rank-and-file of the Labour movement rallied to the call "the Men of Munich must go." The demand was taken up by the delegate meeting of the National Union of Railwaymen and by the district committees of the A.E.U. in such key munitions centres as London, Sheffield, Glasgow and Birmingham. It brought a remarkable trade union response to a conference called on July 7 by the Hammersmith Borough Trades Council and Labour Party, which was promptly disaffiliated by the Labour Party Executive for its effort. So unexpectedly large was the attendance that the Holborn Hall could not contain it and even the Conway Hall, hastily hired, could not accommodate all the overflow. Mr D.N. Pritt got an ovation for his indictment of the Munichites and the Labour leaders who were sheltering them on the "no recriminations" plea; he stressed that it was necessary to look beyond their removal to the formation of "a new Government really representative of the people, based on the rapidly growing movement in the unions and workshops." The conference elected a People's

Vigilance Committee to further the campaign.

Local Labour bodies from Birmingham, Stockport, York, and many points in Scotland and the London suburbs recorded their support for the campaign as the war situation grew more tense. Italy's entry into the war was quickly followed by the first shots of the battle for Africa. An emergency Budget introduced the purchase tax and imposed other heavy burdens on the people. The war in the air began seriously with raids on coastal towns and the opening of the Battle of Britain, which seriously dislocated "Operation Sealion" (the Germans' invasion plan). The future line-up was indicated when Japan formally joined the Axis and Britain received 50 old destroyers from the U.S. in return for the long-term concession of naval and air bases.

During August the air raids on this country grew in frequency and strength, though they were only a foretaste of what was to come. Day by day the *Daily Worker* made big play with the demand for proper shelters and for the use of the warning sirens (the warning system had been suspended, on the strange theory that this would obviate interruption of production). But then on the brilliant, sunny Saturday of September 7 came the first mass raid on to the heart of the capital, the opening of the 57 successive nights of blast and fire, death and destruction, of the London blitz. When the "all clear" blew with the Sunday dawn the East End and Dockside were a shambles. The first casualty list, of over 2,000 dead and seriously wounded, provided its own comment on the miserable inadequacy of the protection available. Nor, in the first numbing shock of that monstrous attack, were there serious efforts to alleviate the sufferings of the homeless. To both problems, which rapidly became nation-wide with the murderous shattering of towns like Coventry and Plymouth and the blitzing of all the big seaports and the main industrial centres, the *Daily Worker* gave redoubled treatment, in the sharpest and most insistent terms.

From the beginning of October this daily drive for serious A.R.P. brought the paper into bitter conflict with Herbert Morrison, who succeeded Anderson as Home Secretary as part of a Cabinet reshuffle. Mr. Morrison, who surpassed his predecessor in his denunciation of deep shelters, hated to be reminded by the *Daily Worker* that "out of office he was all for a '100 per cent. bomb-proof shelter.'" He hated it so much that he went much further than Sir John had ever done and violently attacked deep shelter advocates as "foolish and wicked," "fifth columnists," etc. But he was silent over the real issue which, as the *Daily Worker* pointed out (leader, November 4, 1940) was the utilising of every moment to provide effective civilian shelter; not necessarily deep shelters but at least the concrete shelter recommended by the experts of the A.R.P. Co-ordinating Committee, popularly called the "Haldane."

The *Daily Worker* itself was soon to be a sufferer from the blitz. Dislocation of power and gas supply was so severe in the early days that on three occasions in September the paper could only produce four-page issues, and even those required infinite resource and ingenuity. The four-pager of September 10 was got out in a few thousand copies only on a flat-bed machine; "but still we came out," wrote William Rust the next day, "proof of the fighting spirit of the workers' Press." The four-pager of September 18 carried the news that alternative printing arrangements had had to be operated: "compositors and editorial staff were rushed miles across London at a moment's notice. Machinery and type was transferred. Talk about 'go to it.' A sight to make Herbert Morrison's mouth water!" For the issue of Saturday, September 21, linotypes had to be turned by hand and their pots heated by Primus and blow lamp; the only working light came from pocket torches. On one occasion there was a direct hit at the back of the Cayton Street building. Members of the staff toiled all night through continued raids to save the main rotary motor from being flooded by the firehose water that poured into our machine-room basement.

To the front-line working-class centres of Britain now came a rousing call for further action to organise the fight for a People's Government. The Vigilance Committee set up in July had taken the initiative in launching a call for a People's Convention, to meet in London on January 12, 1941. Over 500 trade unionists, co-operators, Labour men and women, shop stewards, local councillors, scientists, lawyers and artists from all over the country signed the call, which was featured in the *Daily Worker* of September 28.

But while this "true movement of the people," as we called it, began to attract ever-widening support, the reactionary Labour leaders sprung another attack on our paper. The General Council took the unprecedented step of refusing the *Daily Worker* representatives admission to the Press table at the Southport Trades Union Congress, opening on October 7. It was made plain that the Citrine libel action was the ground for this extraordinary decision, the Council apparently taking the vindictive and un-English view that one could be punished twice for the same offence. Sir Walter himself justified the Council in a speech of remarkable bitterness and venom. The Mineworkers and the National Union of Journalists sought in vain to secure a reversal of this decision. In the debate Mr. Smart, of the Building Trade Workers, put his finger prophetically on the spot when he said that the Council's action "constitutes not only a vicious attack upon the freedom of the Press, but the signal for further attacks by the Government against the working class, its Press and its organisations.... Congress is being asked to become the instrument of the Government whereby Mr. Morrison can achieve what Sir John Anderson failed to accomplish, namely, an attack upon a working-class newspaper."

Yet the *Daily Worker,* which had long before shown that it throve on attacks, was in fact on the verge of its greatest achievement since its foundation. That was the printing and publication of a Scottish edition in Scotland; simultaneous printing in two centres, a luxury of the Press lords, had never before been attempted by a working-class newspaper. Great enthusiasm greeted the first appearance of the Scottish *Daily Worker,* from its plant in Glasgow, on Monday, November 11 (the date, by an apt historical irony, when the paper reported the death of Chamberlain—unhonoured, if not exactly unsung).

The new venture was greeted by so distinguished a representative of Scots national life and culture as Sir Hugh Roberton, the famous musician, and snarled at by Glasgow's then Lord Provost, the Labourite P.J. (shortly to become Sir Patrick) Dollan. So enthused were the readers—and by no means only in Scotland—that the Fund, which in September and October had already soared well over £3,000, leapt up in November to no less than £4,261. "We got the news of the final total while still at work," wrote a London factory worker. "You should have heard the cheer that went up in our shop. The foreman thought the war had ended." Even in December, with the customary Christmas slackening, the total reached was £3,727, of which the imposing amount of £1,309 was rushed in in one day, the 31st.

Bill Shepherd, formerly our chief sub-editor and news editor in London, went to Glasgow as editor-in-charge, with J. James, of the Cayton Street composing room, as printer. The pair of them directed prodigies of effort on a flat-bed plant that the average newspaper would have thought impossible; but even with this slow and relatively primitive printing nightly editions of 12,000 to 14,000 were got out, with some three hours' advantage in news deadline. No wonder our eleventh birthday issue (January 1, 1941), describing 1940 as "our greatest year … of spirited advance, of hard battling, of test and trial," should specially select the Scottish *Daily Worker* as "our greatest triumph." "It is precisely this achievement on the Clyde that has called forth the venom of our enemies. Success begets danger. The *Daily Worker* should have died as a result of wartime conditions. Instead of dying, it has given birth."

As 1940 drew to its lurid close the growth of the Convention movement was daily front-page news for us. The Luftwaffe still raged over London—the City had its most devastating fire raid on December 29—and was delivering heavy blows at Birmingham, Bristol, Liverpool, Southampton and other cities. Food and fuel shortages were beginning to make themselves felt as shipping losses grew. No less than five million workers were embraced by wage movements. And it was the workers in the factories who were notably turning to the Convention. This was a highly disagreeable prospect for the ruling class, which intensified its attacks on the Convention and the newspaper that campaigned for it.

Once again the Kemsley Press was to the fore, snarling at the Convention in its biggest provincial sheets (like the Manchester *Daily Dispatch*) and calling for its prohibition. Sir George Broadbridge, M.P. for the City of London, asserted that he had inspired Sir John Anderson's threat of the previous July and declared "it is an absolute enigma to me why the Government hesitates to suppress the *Daily Worker*." In the House of Commons on December 10, Lord Winterton and Mr. Beverley Baxter (then Lord Kemsley's chief editorial adviser) called for the suppression of the paper. On December 20 Mr. Herbert Morrison attacked the Convention as "Communist" and hinted that he might ban it under the Defence Regulations.

But the People's Convention met after all on January 12, overflowing the big hall of the Royal Hotel to fill two others. That was on the Sunday; the previous day's *Daily Worker* was a special eve-of-Convention issue for which a wide and successful sales drive was organised. On the Monday Frank Pitcairn's report of the Convention, leading the paper, commented that the gathering "proved itself even greater than its most ardent supporters could have hoped, or its most bitter enemies feared. It surpassed all expectations alike in size, in character, and in deep impressiveness. No one present yesterday could be in doubt that this event is something great in the history of this country—a beginning of still greater things to come." The opening speeches came from D.N. Pritt, Harry Adams (now President of the A.U.B.T.W.*), the Convention chairman, and the late W.J.R. Squance (former general secretary of the Locomotive Engineers and Firemen). There were 2,234 delegates representing 1,284,000 workers; they included 665 delegates from 497 trade union organisations and 471 delegates from 239 factories.

These were the men and women who acclaimed the Convention's practical eight-point programme for a People's Government and a People's Peace ("won by the working people of all countries and based on the right of all peoples to determine their own destiny"—a peace "neither of conquest nor of capitulation," as Mr. Pritt put it), the other specific points including "to raise the living standards of the people, including wages," "restoration, safeguarding and extension of all trade union rights, and

..................................................

* The Amalgamated Union of Building Trade Workers, now merged into UCATT.—J.E.

democratic rights and civil liberties," emergency powers to take over banks, land and large-scale industry and transport, to end economic chaos and profiteering, freedom for India and the colonies, friendship with the U.S.S.R.

Without waiting for the publication of the official archives or Mr. Morrison's memoirs, it seems quite safe to assert that at that moment the fate of the *Daily Worker* was finally sealed. If the Convention had been a failure the blow might have been withheld for a while; but the Convention had been far too successful. Who could tell where this first serious mass movement of opposition might lead, with a lively daily paper, which had already contributed so much to its development, as its platform and its organiser? On January 14, 1941, the *Daily Worker* splash told of twelve great regional conferences, covering every part of the country, which the Convention had already scheduled to carry forward the week-end's work. Precisely a week later the blow fell.

In the morning of Tuesday, January 21, Mr. Herbert Morrison, Home Secretary and Minister of Home Security, called the Newspaper Proprietors' Association before him and announced that he had that day issued the necessary Orders under Defence Regulation 2D for the suppression of the *Daily Worker* (with which was coupled *The Week,* the duplicated news-letter issued personally by Claud Cockburn). At 2 o'clock he repeated the announcement to the Editors of national newspapers, who were summoned to the presence for the purpose. Early that evening Det.-Insp. Whitehead, leading a posse of Special Branch men, and supported by uniformed police who surrounded Cayton Street in due form, raided and seized our offices and formally carried out the suppression. There were the usual searches and questionings. And, since Mr. Morrison had thoughtfully added a separate Order under Defence Regulation 94B that the newspaper's rotary presses should be sequestered until leave had been obtained from the High Court, they were sealed and placed under police guard. Parallel operations were carried out the same evening at the offices and plant of the Scottish *Daily Worker* in Glasgow.*

......................................................

* The leader of that last day, headed "We Accuse the Government," proclaimed that the crisis in war production was "due to the reckless profiteering and incompetence of the ruling class," and that the charge against the Communist Party of fomenting strikes and obstructing the war effort was "a fake, deliberately designed to distract attention from the guilty men of capitalism." "The *Daily Worker* can prove that more working hours have been lost in certain factories as a result of mismanagement than in all the strikes of recent months."

## Chapter Eight

# The Fight to Beat the Ban

FOR THE NEXT nineteen months the *Daily Worker*, as a newspaper, did not exist; yet as a political force, temporarily disembodied though it might be, it grew in potency and influence with every week that passed. The fight against the ban made the *Daily Worker* a household word throughout the Labour movement, and in many circles outside. Mr. Morrison and his Transport House and Tory cronies found themselves in the grip of a contradiction from which there was no escape. The more they hardened their hearts and clung obstinately to the ban, hoping that they would thus strangle for good the clear Communist voice of the advanced working people, the wider the sympathetic echoes that voice evoked.

Never before in British history had a newspaper been kept out of action for so long by mere ministerial *diktat*. And yet assuredly the result was far other than that for which the suppressors hoped. The period of the ban brought the *Daily Worker* a wider sympathy and support than it had ever known and paved the way for its subsequent development into a front-rank popular national newspaper of the working class.

The campaign against the ban fell into two principal periods, the German invasion of the Soviet Union on June 22, 1941, being the obvious dividing line. It was an odd reflection on the genuineness of the "systematic opposition to the war" ground for invoking 2D that the second period of the ban was the longest. For no less than 14 months after the war's character had been transformed, and the Communist Party and the *Daily Worker* were in the fullest support, the ban was obdurately maintained.

From the start it was the evoking of Regulation 2D, making the Home Secretary his own judge, jury and executioner, that brought the widest protest. Many persons and organisations who shared Mr. Morrison's hostility to the paper were gravely alarmed by the use of an arbitrary weapon which the Government was thought to have pledged itself only to use in the crisis of actual invasion. Why, it was asked on all sides, was a specific charge not made and those responsible for the paper brought to trial? The late Mr. J. Marchbank, general secretary of the National Union of Railwaymen, summed up this point of view when he wrote: "It would have been infinitely more satisfactory if a charge of this kind had been considered in open court and a judicial decision taken. The action of the Home Office smacks of the Gestapo" (*Railway Review,* January 31, 1941).

At no point did Mr. Morrison face up to this point-blank challenge, put to him formally in a letter from Professor Haldane, as chairman of our Editorial Board, offering to face trial in a court of law if the suppression under 2D were withdrawn. On January 28 he told the House of Commons that to have followed the normal procedure of 2C would have involved a delay of two to four months, "and that would not be government in time of war." Blandly ignoring the power of the Government to secure priority in the courts, Mr. Morrison's sudden passion for extreme urgency invited the acid riposte of the editorial columnist of *Reynolds News* (February 2, 1941) that "speed—in preventing the heart being burned out of London, for example, and in applying compulsory powers to property—is not yet an outstanding virtue of the Government."

But there were further strange contradictions in Mr. Morrison's position. He never explained at all why such dictatorial speed had suddenly become necessary. Indeed, in his initial statement to the House on January 22, he asserted that he had not acted because there had been any recent change or development in the *Daily Worker,* or because of the appearance of any particular articles. The paper, he averred, had been offending since the end of September, 1939, its "settled and continuous policy" being "to weaken the will of our people to achieve victory." Six days later, when the House debated the suppression, his apologia took an even odder twist. He made no attempt to demonstrate that the *Daily Worker* had had any adverse effect on morale; he implied that it had not; but, "looking ahead," he had thought such a result, "sooner or later" … "highly probable." Therefore, smirked this Cockney convert to the old-world Continental principle of preventive arrest, "I came to the conclusion that it was not fair to wait until actual damage to morale had been done, and that it was far better to anticipate the possibility of damage."

That debate of January 28 arose on a motion by Mr. Aneurin Bevan, then a private Labour M.P., and Sir Richard Acland, then Liberal Member for Barnstaple. The motion dissociated its sponsors from the policy of the *Daily Worker,* but protested against the use of 2D. An amendment by Mr. H.B. Lees-Smith, Labour M.P. for Keighley, removed the protest and substituted complete endorsement of the ban. Mr. Bevan sharply criticised the Home Secretary for going behind the back of Parliament while drawing the other newspapers in to "connive" at his unprecedented action. There could be only one explanation of Mr. Morrison's refusal to take the *Daily Worker* to court on a specific charge—he wished to intimidate the Press as a whole.*

For the rest, the debate was remarkable for two more things: an astonishing piece of clowning by Mr. Morrison and a forthright intervention by William Gallacher. The Member for West Fife rammed home the point that the *Daily Worker* had been suppressed on the same day that the Cabinet announced its new measures for industrial conscription, and poured scorn on the Home Secretary's earlier attempts to deny that there was any connection between the two events. Far from menacing morale,

...............................................

* Around this time there was talk at influential levels of the desirability of a drastic reduction in the number of national newspapers, even of the merging of all papers in a single official sheet, like Mr. Churchill's 1926 *British Gazette* of egregious memory. And on February 6, 1941, questions were put in the House—though Mr. Churchill evaded them—about Cabinet threats privately conveyed to the *Daily Mirror* and *Sunday Pictorial* (both those mass tabloids being then distinctly leftist and critical in tone).

the campaigns of the *Daily Worker* had strengthened morale, and the paper stood and fought all the time for the one thing that could raise morale in the fight against Fascism—"a powerful, united, independent working-class movement."

"One of the reasons for its suppression is that the *Daily Worker* has exposed day after day the rotten profiteering and the corruption in the ruling class, especially among the employers, especially when they are paid cost plus.... The *Daily Worker* day after day has exposed the disorganisation of the factories and the fact that it is the employers who are responsible for it and the failure to get effective production."

It must be presumed that Mr. Morrison, in his reply to the debate, embarked on his essay in low comedy by way of diversion; for at no point did he even attempt to traverse, let alone answer, the cogent points put by Mr. Gallacher. But he had some rollicking fun to offer the Tories; and loudly they rose to it. The police report on the suppression, he asserted, revealed that "a real son of the proletariat," in the paper's machine-room, describing the editorial staff with a "big, bad word," had said "twice we went on strike down here to get them to alter something which we would not stand for." Mr. George Isaacs chipped in to say that "as General Secretary of the union to which these people belong I can endorse that. They have stopped publication many times." Mr. Morrison added a roguish and witty reference to the "dictatorship of the proletariat."

To introduce such grotesque prejudice scarcely accorded with

Mr. Morrison's boast that he had handled the affair "judicially and impartially." But it was wonderful copy for the millionaire Press; and a pall of silence was dropped over the aftermath. For three days later the *Daily Worker* Natsopa* machine chapel met, with the only non-member of the chapel on duty on the night of the suppression present (he was a machine-minder), and repudiated Mr. Morrison's statement. The Home Secretary, however, lay low; only after a fortnight had passed was his Under-Secretary put up to say that the chapel repudiation was "valueless and misleading" since the man quoted by the police was not a member of it—suppressing the fact that the only non-member was present at the chapel meeting, a fact duly attested by the Father of the Chapel in a letter of which Mr. Morrison had been sent a copy. It was additionally alleged that the *Daily Worker* had endeavoured to browbeat the Natsopa men into signing a statement, which they had refused to do (this piece of invention was promptly repudiated by Professor Haldane, as Editorial Board chairman).

Mr. George Isaacs, despite the distressing lack of co-ordination between his story and Mr. Morrison's, persisted in his enthusiastic claim that Natsopa members had taken action— strictly forbidden by the newspaper agreement of 1926 which Mr. Isaacs had signed—to enforce editorial changes in the *Daily Worker*. But when directly challenged by Professor Haldane,

..................................................

* The National Society of Operative Printers and Assistants, now, after a series of mergers, part of Unite.—J.E.

in a detailed review of the allegations, to produce particulars he refused to reply, on the singularly lame pretext that if he did it would be "distorted."

The debate of January 28, with the whips on, had given Mr. Morrison his majority—but 11 M.P.s had stood firm while 297 trooped docilely into the Government lobby. And the tide of popular protest had already begun to rise. Sir Richard Acland read to the House a letter he had received from a soldier stationed in his constituency. It read:

"I wish to add my protest and that of many other soldiers against this blow against freedom.... They include friends and opponents of the *Daily Worker* policy, daily readers and people who rarely, if ever, see the paper, Socialists, Liberals and even men who have supported the Conservative Party.... As members of H.M. Army we have been told that we are fighting for freedom and democracy and we are determined that freedom and democracy shall not be sacrificed."

The fact was that masses of people, speaking through scores (soon hundreds) of public meetings, resolutions from Trades Councils, union branches and union Executives—the Railwaymen and the South Wales miners were first off the mark—grasped the point put by William Rust in a letter to the *News Chronicle* (January 28, 1941): "the charge of being unpatriotic, defeatist and subversive is all too frequently employed in order to stir up wartime emotions against those awkward critics who use the kind of spotlight which exposes profiteers, industrial chaos and crooked imperialist intrigues." And in the first detailed statement they issued immediately after the suppression (*The Case for the "Daily Worker"*) the Editorial Board put the same fundamental point from the positive angle: "The *Daily Worker* has always fought for the independence and liberty of the British people, it will fight to the last ditch against their subjugation by any foreign imperialism just as it fights against the ruling class at home which is exploiting the war for its own selfish and anti-social interests."

Mr. Morrison had indeed managed to "co-ordinate" the Press very well, so far as its editorial columns were concerned. On January 22 the value of the previous afternoon's confidential chat with editors was seen; with the exception of the *Daily Mirror,* which had the best of reasons to be alarmed at a "dangerous precedent," every leading article endorsed the suppression; even the Liberal *News Chronicle*—which was later to develop very serious qualms—cheered Herbert on in a ponderous and very smug double-column leader entitled "The End of the Rope." But the letter columns told a different story. A survey of the national daily and Sunday papers, and the leading provincials, showed over 100 letters from readers on the *Daily Worker* ban; and the proportion of ban-opponents to ban-supporters was approximately 7-4.

The extent of these protests was significant. The Executive of the National Council for Civil Liberties, with Professor Harold Laski, Mr. Kingsley Martin (Editor of the *New Statesman and Nation*) and Lord Faringdon among those present, met immediately and expressed its "deep sense of disturbance"; in a more detailed statement later the Council noted particularly that, since Mr. Morrison had been one of the *Daily Worker's* principal ministerial targets, it was particularly objectionable that he should "by choosing to act under Regulation 2D, in effect suppress without the right of appeal the expression of grievances against his own policies." Sharp words also came from outstanding intellectual leaders like Bernard Shaw,* H.G. Wells, Henry W. Nevinson, Professor Berriedale Keith (the most eminent authority on the constitutional law of the Empire) and Lord Ponsonby.

That out of the first spontaneous protests there then developed a massive nation-wide political campaign was above all due to the soundness of that "steel framework" of which Rust had spoken

........................................

* Shaw's protest (*Labour Monthly,* March 1941) is worth quoting. He observed that the *Daily Worker* and *The Week* "were suppressed, not for saying the things that all the other papers were saying as well, but for very wisely grasping the fact that a good understanding with Russia is all-important to us; for a war between the U.S.S.R and the British Commonwealth would make every intelligent Briton a defeatist. Civilisation would be really at stake in it, with the Commonwealth on the wrong side." Shaw added that Professor Haldane and Claud Cockburn, "persons of unquestionable mental capacity and knowledge of the modern world, knew this and ran their papers accordingly. The War Cabinet, a coalition of Old School Ties and trade unionists, does not know it; it nurses a blind hatred of Russia because private property, with its sequel of idle parasitism and poverty, has been abolished there, all property being held subject to the public welfare.... It would have been far more sensible to suppress *The Times* and all the other papers which have for years carried on, and are still carrying on, a campaign of insult, calumny and clamour for a capitalist united front against Bolshevism."

a year before—the *Daily Worker* Leagues (they now added the word "Defence" to their title). The Leagues were the heart and soul of the fight, and their national organiser, George Allison, its indefatigable director. By the late spring Allison was able to report that the Leagues had 160 local committees, organised on a factory or area basis, with 60 Bazaar groups working to raise money for the Fund. That famous institution, far from succumbing with the paper it had nourished, found new scope, new form as a trust fund—and a new name that was to stay: the People's Press Fighting Fund. Throughout the period of the ban the Fund, which organised a weekly circularisation of 4,500 groups and individual supporters, successfully raised the indispensable sinews of the campaign, to the tune of over £1,000 a month—the total sum for the period being £23,186.

Some index of the intensity of the campaign against the ban, even in its opening stages, can be gathered from these statistics: during its first three months over 750,000 leaflets were distributed and over 250,000 pamphlets and other publications sold. It was early recognised that to attempt to produce an "illegal" *Daily Worker* would be pointless and would indeed hamstring the mass campaign for the lifting of the ban. A couple of "illegal" duplicated issues were run off in the first days of the ban, but even as a demonstration their effect was negligible. On the other hand, a group of former members of the staff started a small news agency which issued a daily news bulletin under the title *Industrial and General Information,* with the special aim of maintaining—even though for a limited subscription readership of local working-class leaders—the exclusive news service that the *Daily Worker* had developed. The police at first probed rather persistently into this venture, with which Walter Holmes was particularly associated, apparently thinking it might be a formal breach of the ban. On March 16, 1941, the I.G.I. offices were raided and searched, but nothing transpired.

Meantime the air blitz continued to rock Britain, and in March and April London had some of its heaviest-ever raids. The two big April raids were so severe that Londoners still speak of them shortly as "the Wednesday" and "the Saturday." On "the Wednesday" (April 16, 1941) the Luftwaffe finished the job Morrison had begun. The City Road area was heavily bombed and the *Daily Worker's* offices and plant in Cayton Street totally destroyed by fire. The story is best told in a contemporary leaflet by William Rust, headed "Bombed and Banned":

"The building, originally a tea warehouse, had wide timber floors and very little steel work. It burnt like a match box, despite the heroic efforts of the staff present (two firewatchers, the regular night watchman and two machine-men) to stem the flames. Bombs had been raining down since 9.30 p.m., and the incendiary bomb which finally struck the building fell at 1.30 a.m. It lodged in a space between partition walls, where it was inaccessible. Firemen arrived on the scene, struggling bravely with the difficulties of water supply, in a narrow street where flames spouted from side to side. Local people, citizens of Hoxton and St. Luke's, bore a hand, although their own defenceless homes were threatened. But all the efforts to save the building were in vain. There is little or nothing to salvage from these ruins of what was once a highly efficient printing plant valued at £60-£70,000. No compensation will be paid by the Government until after the war." [It has not been paid yet.—G.A.H.]

Most embittering was the thought that the sequestering of the rotary presses under Regulation 94B had prevented the removal of any of these then totally irreplaceable and enormously costly machines to a place of safety. The necessary application had been duly made to the High Court, but that august body did not hand down its decision till April 22, five days after the machines had been reduced to twisted scrap. It then agreed that the machines could be released.

Before those Cayton Street bombs fell the Editorial Board had made a new approach to Mr. Morrison. That was on April 4; a reasoned case for the lifting of the ban was submitted in the form of a lengthy memorandum, traversing the various grounds of the Government's case, and stressing particularly that the *Daily Worker's* "record both before and during the war is a testimony to its consistent anti-Fascism. It is unalterably opposed to any measures that would weaken the capacity of the British people to defend themselves against German imperialism." The Home Secretary's reply was not vouchsafed until he had had the satisfaction of knowing that the paper's entire printing resources were in ruins. On April 18 he returned the pontifical response: "the reasons for which it was found necessary to take action under the Regulation have lost none of their force in the period which has elapsed since the paper was suppressed."

The general situation of the war was growing every day more tense by the late spring of 1941. It was, in fact, approaching its tremendous turning-point; for, as we now know, Hitler had given orders for the preparation of Plan Barbarossa—the invasion of the Soviet Union—at the end of 1940. In the Balkans and Libya the Germans took the initiative. Yugoslavia was attacked (but with a significant immediate response in the beginnings of popular resistance over the heads of the treacherous ruling clique). In Greece and Libya strong German armies reinforced the wilting Italians and drove back the British forces; the disaster of Crete was at hand.

What was the reverse side of the picture? The U.S.S.R. had concluded a treaty with Yugoslavia at the very moment of the German attack. In May, Stalin himself took over the Soviet Premiership. London politicians plunged into excited speculation. Sir Stafford Cripps was sent as Ambassador to Moscow, enough of the myth of his militancy still clinging to him to delude many people into thinking this was a serious political gesture. But at the highest level the note remained the defensive—and delay. Mr. Churchill forever postponed the hour of decision; at the end of 1940 he spoke of 1941, in 1941 he looked forward to 1942; it was always "next year ... next year," so that the cynics might be forgiven for catching an echo "sometime ... never." It was hardly surprising that, on the eve of the fatal throw, Hitler's deputy Hess should have made his fantastic solo flight to these shores hoping that the dark forces among the British ruling class might yet be rallied for the war against Bolshevism.

There was indeed an ancient and French-like smell about our upper circles in those days; not least of its symptoms was the news blackout which made newspaper columns a mockery and began to spread serious alarm and despondency. The public even started to turn to the German Radio for news. Informed people admitted that the Government's arbitrary removal of the one opposition paper was the main factor in this serious situation. "The suppression of the *Daily Worker* may or may not have weakened the influence of the Communist Party," wrote Mr. G.R. Strauss, M.P., "but it certainly has had a most serious effect on the independence of the Press as a whole." Widespread concern was reflected in the conference on Freedom of the Press called jointly by the National Union of Journalists and the National Council for Civil Liberties on June 7. This broad gathering united 1,011 delegates from 616 organisations with a membership of over 1¼ million. It demanded a more rational censorship, the ending of 2D, and the lifting of the ban on the *Daily Worker*.

Highly effective play was made of the "Battle of the News" in the *People's Press Special,* first of the beat-the-ban broadsheets, issued in May, 1941. The Special also disclosed that the movement against the ban had already embraced over a million trade unionists, protest resolutions having come from more than 800 local and district union bodies, Trades Councils, factory organisations, Labour Parties and the like. Nearly a million engineers, the shock troops of war production, were to be added to that host when the National Committee of the Amalgamated Engineering Union voted by no less than 43 to 4 for the lifting of the ban.

That was the position when, early on the brilliant Sunday morning of June 22, the world shook to the news of the perfidious German invasion of Russia. Mr. Churchill rose to the occasion in his famous broadcast that evening, in effect greeting the U.S.S.R. as an ally and scotching the hopes of the Hess-ites. It was one of the supreme moments of world history, the "climacteric," as Churchill called it, of the war. Literally overnight everything had been changed. And how could capitalist Britain stand shoulder to shoulder with Communist Russia against the common enemy of mankind and still maintain an arbitrary ban on Britain's only Communist daily newspaper? The point was seized by Professor Haldane in an immediate telegram to the Prime Minister: "In view of your statement re turning point of war and tasks of all free peoples, ask you consider immediate withdrawal of order suppressing *Daily Worker*."*

But the old lion lay very low and left the *Daily Worker* to his shadier Tory and Social-Democratic jackals, with the ineffable

...........................................

* This was followed up by a specific declaration, in July, that a re-issued *Daily Worker* would "(1) Give its full support to the Government and do everything possible to strengthen British-Soviet unity in the fight to bring about a people's victory over German Fascism; (2) Direct its influence in the factories, mines and trade unions towards securing the maximum production for victory; (3) Handle international affairs from the standpoint of encouraging the liberation fight of the people in the countries enslaved by German Fascism"

Mr. Morrison as leader of the pack. Weeks, then months, passed and there was no sign of any Cabinet move for the lifting of the ban. The Executive Committee of the South Wales Miners' Federation asked the Home Secretary to receive a deputation but were curtly rebuffed. There was indeed reason for the sharp Press statement by William Rust on July 3 that "there are quite a number of would-be quislings in high places whose influence is directed against the re-publication of the *Daily Worker,* just as they are hostile to a real policy of co-operation with the Soviet Union. Since the banning of the *Daily Worker* they have enjoyed their immunity from criticism, and their opposition to the lifting of the ban is quite understandable."

The campaign for the *Daily Worker* had now been elevated by events to the plane of top-level politics; at all points it was integrated with the fundamental issues of universal war against Fascism: (1) the Second Front; (2) production; (3) national unity. Precisely on these points the Communist Party, recruiting rapidly to the record membership of 50,000, developed a practical and positive campaign which had a deep political effect throughout the working-class movement, and beyond. Speeches by Harry Pollitt received nation-wide publicity (even on the B.B.C.), were praised by the Press as "vigorous and sensible"—in contrast to the cheap anti-Communism of certain union leaders (e.g., the unlamented Mr. George Gibson, presiding at the Edinburgh T.U.C. in September, 1941). But, as Pollitt told a London demonstration on June 26, referring to the *Daily Worker* ban, "at this moment we are compelled to fight with one of our most powerful weapons taken away from us."

In August, William Rust summed up the position in an article in the *Labour Monthly* entitled "The *Daily Worker* and the National Front." The "enormous and spontaneous strengthening of the demand for the lifting of the ban" was exemplified in forthright statements from personalities like the Bishop of Bradford, J.B. Priestley, Augustus John; in the increase of national trade unions against the ban to sixteen; in the passage of anti-ban resolutions by thirty co-operative societies with an aggregate membership of over one million. "We are so confident," Rust wrote, "that the raising of the ban cannot be long avoided that the necessary arrangements have already been made for the printing of the paper." Formerly hostile newspapers, led by the *News Chronicle* and the *Manchester Guardian,* now gave editorial support to the campaign against the ban.

But there could be little doubt that hope long deferred was making the hearts of many *Daily Worker* supporters very sick. And it is to the eternal credit of William Rust that at this trying moment he never lost heart or enthusiasm; instead, he stepped up the campaign for sustained and extended mass pressure to new heights. Every month of the latter half of 1941 saw a new broadsheet "Special," *For Victory Over Fascism, British Worker, Workers' News* (which sold over 400,000), the *Worker, New Year Clarion.* The Specials,* produced on the press of a country weekly by Archie Bassett and Fred Asten, now works manager

---

* The Specials reached an aggregate circulation of 2,000,000 copies.

and printer of the *Daily Worker,* have a saga all of their own, of continuous day and night working under seemingly impossible technical conditions. To back them, for the leading folk, there appeared from July, 1941, to March, 1942, thirty-two numbers of a weekly pocket-size *Commentary on Current Political Events* in an average print of 7,000 copies; here the political and strategic case for striking in the West was cogently argued. Of meetings there was no end, the summation of them all being the monster London gathering in the Stoll Theatre, addressed by miners' and railwaymen's leaders, on November 30.

On the production front the enormous possibilities awaiting the real enthusing of manpower were strikingly demonstrated when, in September, Lord Beaverbrook as Minister of Production proclaimed a Tanks-for-Russia week. Never had the armament factories seen such output, such labour enthusiasm among men and women, young and old. Echoes of that week were still strong when the Engineering and Allied Trades Shop Stewards' National Council called a national conference on production. Meeting in London on October 19, that conference was attended by 1,237 delegates from some 300 key war factories—including the most famous in the country—representing half a million workers. "Work and fight" was the slogan of this remarkable gathering, one of the most remarkable of the whole war, with its demand for a real production drive, its reports of labour initiative and heroism—and the thunderous applause with which it greeted the demand for the lifting of the ban on the *Daily Worker.* "We believe," said the conference resolution simply, "that this paper can help us a lot in carrying through the policy of this conference for increased production."

But more and more, through all the other associated issues, it became plain that the central political question, the acid test of the genuineness of the Anglo-Soviet Alliance, was the Second Front in Europe. This was clearly recognised by the dark forces of reaction who concentrated all their powers of sabotage here. Nothing was too small, nothing was too large, for these influential elements who from the beginning set themselves to "hint a doubt and hesitate dislike" of Britain's mighty Socialist Ally. The Foreign Office blimps made themselves the laughing-stock of the country by refusing to let the B.B.C. add the "International" to the Allied anthems, even after the signing of the first Anglo-Soviet agreement on July 12. The War Office "experts" asserted that the Russian war would be all over in six weeks. Lord Wavell's profound strategic appreciation was contained in the words "chiefly it has given us a lull to re-equip and rest." And this poisonous nonsense had spread to leading circles of the Labour movement; in its first editorial reaction the *Daily Herald* (June 24) wrote "let us not indulge premature hopes of successful Russian resistance. Our evidence of Russian armed strength is scanty. Such as there is discourages extravagant optimism."*

* On January 27, 1942, Mr. Churchill was to declare in the House of Commons that the Soviet military successes were "unhoped for, undreamed of by us, because we little knew the Russian strength." In the same debate Mr. Noel Baker spoke of "the disastrous advice which we received about the power of Russia to resist." There was grim point in the wisecrack in our Commentary

The cat was let well out of the bag by Colonel J.T.C. Moore-Brabazon (later Lord Brabazon), Minister of Aircraft Production. In a private talk with representatives of the industry he blandly advanced the view that it would be a good thing for Germany and Russia to destroy each other so that Britain would become the dominant power in Europe. Jack Tanner, of the A.E.U., made a great sensation at the Edinburgh T.U.C. in 1941 when he disclosed this "indiscretion"—as it was at once officially labelled—of Brabazon's. But the whole trend of subsequent events indicated that what this pre-war friend of Mosley's had so indiscreetly blurted out was a true reflex of the inner policy of the British ruling class, not excluding Churchill himself.

It was symbolic that the categorical statement that there would be no Second Front in 1941, giving the Nazis the green light for their tremendous drive on Moscow and their preparations for the spring offensive, was made by the old Municheer and Chamberlainite, Lord Halifax, then Ambassador in Washington. On the other hand, the official sneer that all Second Fronters were "armchair strategists" received a rude shock when, in his Revolution anniversary address in November, Stalin himself put the case for the Second Front—at the very moment when, as Supreme Commander-in-Chief, he was preparing and directing

........................................

(No. 18, December 3, 1941): "What is a military expert? Answer: a military expert is a man who, having predicted that the Maginot Line was invincible and that the Red Army would collapse in two weeks, now expects you to take his word that a Second Front in Europe is impossible."

the first great Soviet counter-offensive which hurled the Germans back from the gates of Moscow and resounded through the world as the first massive defeat of the Wehrmacht.

The New Year opened to new and stupendous shocks. The policy of the "sitzkrieg" had encouraged the Japanese to launch their joint attack on Britain and the U.S., which was thus at last brought into the general war. The shameful disaster of Malaya and Singapore, with the threat to Burma and India, was at hand. There was dismay and bitterness among the people. Our Editorial Board once more approached the Home Secretary, repeating their July declaration, and making the sensible point that "whatever differences existed between the *Daily Worker* and other sections of popular opinion on the ways and means of carrying on the fight against Fascism, we are happy to say that they now belong to the past." But Mr. Morrison was living in the past. *London News,* the Labour Party organ specially his very own, shortly came out with a violent tirade against the *Daily Worker,* based on two-year-old quotations; and Transport House had the article reprinted as a leaflet for mass distribution. Alas, poor Herbert! Even in his own constituency of Hackney a public ballot was to record 6,698 for lifting the ban and only 280 for keeping it on.

Events were now beginning to move too fast for these Tory and Transport House diehards. Mr. Eden returned from an official visit to Moscow speaking as a man upon whom a great light has fallen; and *The Times* (December 30, 1941) commented that "men of vision cannot fail to see that humanity is passing through the fire of social revolution as well as of universal war, and that the world which will emerge from the ordeal will in many respects think and believe and act very differently from the world of the past." A Soviet trade union delegation, headed by Mr. Shvernik, arrived here following the earlier conclusion of an agreement between the T.U.C. and the All-Union Central Council of Trade Unions; its tour of the country was described by the *Daily Herald* in terms of a triumphal progress. What he called a "disconcerted" tribute to popular feeling was paid by ex-diplomat Harold Nicolson: "one has only to mention Russia," he said, "and the whole meeting flames as suddenly as a wisp of hay drenched in paraffin. One feels upon one's cheek the wind of the wings of passion."

In the spring Lord Beaverbrook launched an individual and cogent call for a Second Front which was echoed through all his newspapers and which evoked a remarkable response in America; it was later to transpire that the highest American political and military opinion favoured a Second Front in 1942, but was choked off by Churchill. Simultaneously it was learned that the *Daily Mirror* had been warned that it might be suppressed under 2D—ostensibly because of a bitter cartoon on shipping losses,* but actually because it and its stable companion, the *Sunday Pictorial,* were employing their mammoth circulations to put

..............................................

* Philip Zec's famous cartoon showing a shipwrecked sailor clinging to a piece of wreckage, with the caption: "'The price of petrol has been increased by one penny—official.'—J.E.

over a generally left critical line and had sharply campaigned for the Second Front.

Under bold slogans: "Victory this Year," "Time Our Blows with Theirs," "Attack! Attack! Attack!" the Communist Party put out its greatest mobilisation as the spearhead of the *Daily Worker* campaign. On March 21 the vast Central Hall, Westminster, was packed out with 1,903 delegates from 645 London organisations and 177 factories; to their reiterated demand for the lifting of the ban came with sensational political effect this message from Lloyd George, no less: "the continued suppression of the *Daily Worker* is an act of stupid and wanton partisan spite and of sheer despotism. No wonder there still remains a trace of suspicion in Russia as to the wholehearted genuineness of our co-operation."*

Those biting and apt words of the Liberal Elder Statesman echoed through the whole Labour movement. The Liberal M.P.s requested their leader, Sir Archibald Sinclair, to raise the question of the *Daily Worker* ban in the Cabinet. And then on May 28, in the teeth of their own Executive's contrary recommendation, the Labour Party conference, sweeping aside the antique quotation-chopping and anti-Communist platitudes of the late James Walker (Iron and Steel Trades, M.P. for Motherwell), voted for

* Mr. Morrison was extremely put out by the publicity this conference received. The present writer, then night editor of *Reynolds News,* gave big play to the conference, leading with the Lloyd George message. Mr. Morrison wrote a personal letter of angry protest to Mr. Sydney Elliott, then *Reynolds* editor.

the lifting of the ban by 1,244,000 to 1,231,000. This repudiation of Mr. Morrison by his own Party received a tremendous Press, and it might have been thought that all was now over. Not so.

Within a few days the public announcement was made of the signing in London, by Mr. Molotov and Mr. Eden, of a 20-year Treaty of Alliance between Britain and the U.S.S.R. The announcement contained the key sentence "in the course of the negotiations complete agreement was reached between the two countries with regard to the urgent tasks of the creation of a Second Front in Europe in 1942." The tasks were indeed urgent. Profiting by the absence of a Second Front, the Germans had mounted their gigantic summer offensive, to carry them through the Ukraine and the Kuban to the Caucasus foothills, to take Sevastopol and Odessa, to tighten the steel ring round Leningrad, and to sweep over the steppe to the Volga at Stalingrad.

But although the military position of Britain was also very grave—Rommel was forging ahead rapidly in Libya, and Tobruk fell in June—the saboteurs of the Second Front did not relax their efforts. The fantastic theory that the war could be won by long-distance mass bombing of German cities came into its own with the first giant raid, by 1,000 planes on Cologne in June. So serious was the situation by mid-July that the March *Daily Worker* conference was recalled, a Second Front demonstration planned for Trafalgar Square on Sunday, July 26 (organised in one week it gathered over 60,000 Londoners to voice the demand for action) and a National Deputations Day to M.P.s on July 29.

Deputations Day turned out one of the most remarkable pieces of mass lobbying the House of Commons had ever seen. There were at least 1,500 delegates from nearly 350 constituencies. With them they took copies of the *Daily* —— (the *Daily Blank* it was speedily christened), a four-page full specimen newspaper showing what the *Daily Worker* would have been like if it had appeared the previous day. The leading article, entitled "Stalingrad," asked "how long will it take until both people and Government fully realise that the fate of Britain is being decided on the banks of the Don and the Volga?" and concluded, "Stalingrad will not be given up. It will be defended by the full might of the Red Army. The defence of Stalingrad will be Britain's opportunity this year just as the defence of Moscow was our opportunity last. We must not fail a second time."

There was not now very much hope for Mr. Morrison. The Co-operative Congress, with its 8,700,000 membership, had condemned the use of 2D and demanded the annulment of the Regulation. Trade Union support for the lifting of the ban had now embraced over 50 national unions, with a membership approaching 3,000,000. Out of the Big Five unions that dominate the T.U.C., Mr. Morrison could now only count on two, the general labour Unions. The Scottish Trades Union Congress had passed a resolution against the ban. And the T.U.C. itself was meeting at Blackpool in the second week of September; there was no sort of doubt that it would carry a lift-the-ban resolution by a much larger majority than the Labour Party conference. The *Daily Worker* Leagues were putting out their biggest effort in a campaign leading up to the T.U.C. to make sure that any last-minute chicane by Transport House would be fruitless.

So, late in the afternoon of Wednesday, August 26, 1942, a Home Office messenger appeared at the Southampton Row offices of the *Daily Worker* Leagues bearing a letter signed by Mr. Morrison's Deputy Under-Secretary, Sir Frank Newsam, K.B.E., C.V.O., M.C. (salary £2,200). The Editorial Board were thereby officially informed that the Home Secretary "has this day revoked the Order, etc., etc." … The ban was lifted.

## Chapter Nine
# Back into Action

THE REPUBLICATION OF the *Daily Worker* on September 7, 1942, was a truly great day in the history of the British working class and its Press; for the paper itself it was the climax of a ten days' wonder. The lifting of the ban found us without staff—12 of our 18 journalists were in the Forces—without a printing plant, and without any capital. Despite their lines of idle machines, neither the Press monopolists nor the big newspaper printers would touch us, though offered the most favourable contract terms; even the Rt. Hon. Alfred Barnes, M.P., then chairman of the Co-operative Press, Ltd., whose printing staff would have been most happy to handle us, proved entirely unco-operative. Fortunately it was discovered that B.I.S.A.K.T.A. (the iron and steel trade union) was anxious to dispose of its old-established printing works, the London Caledonian Press, in Swinton Street, Gray's Inn Road, which had a twenty-year-old rotary once used to print the *Workers' Weekly* and the *Sunday Worker*. Within eighteen hours a deal was put through and a call launched to our supporters to raise £50,000, the major part of this sum being the purchase price of the "Cale." It was the surest sign of the surging support for the revived *Daily Worker,* and one of the proudest achievements of our whole history, that this amount was raised in a little over three months, by December 5. It was also a remarkable personal achievement for George Allison, who took over the Fund from Violet Lansbury at this moment, and who was able in his turn—on leaving us for leading Communist Party work—to hand over in December to Barbara Niven with such a grand beginning.

But the acquisition of the Caledonian Press was not the end of our technical problems. Far from it. The rotary plant had not worked regularly since the *Sunday Worker* ceased publication in 1929 (old *Sunday Worker* formes were actually found when we started cleaning up the composing room*). Engineers and printers had a herculean job cleaning, preparing and testing machinery. There were only six vintage linotypes, three stuck right away at the other end of the works, none of them properly equipped with modern matrices (not till October 1 could the paper appear in an up-to-date text dress). Sub-editors and reporters were jammed into two tiny rooms, with the Editor and his secretary in a partitioned off space hardly more than a large cupboard. Things improved as time went on, of course; but to the end of its days in Swinton Street the *Daily Worker*

........................................

* In the pre-computer days typesetting was a task needing large amounts of skilled manual labour. Pages were set in the composing room with a linotype, an intricate machine which produced a line of type at a time using a special keyboard, a magazine full of metal letter moulds and a cauldron of molten lead. These strips of lead were assembled in a frame called a chase to make up a forme, or ready-to-print page.—J.E.

was cribb'd, cabin'd and confin'd—more particularly in that key department, the composing room—in a way that no daily newspaper has ever been.

As to the editorial staffing problem it is enough to say that of the 22 who were hastily gathered together only 11 had had any newspaper experience (six on national newspapers); of nine sub-editors only four had had any newspaper experience (two on nationals), none of it at sub-editing! The writer of these lines, who secured release from the night editorship of *Reynolds News* to become our chief sub-editor, was the sole experienced member of the sub-editorial staff. So green, in fact, were our subs that within a few weeks it was necessary to prepare a printed elementary textbook for them. Entitled "Notes for *Daily Worker* Sub-Editors," commonly called "the Subs' Bible," this little work incidentally became the talk of the trade, and is believed to be quite a collectors' item in Fleet Street. Typical of the staff difficulties of the time was the fact that Alan Winnington, later (1948-9) our special correspondent with the Liberation Armies in China, had to be trained to the exacting and expert job of deputy chief sub in a fortnight.

Among outstanding additions were J.R. Campbell as assistant editor and industrial editor, Ivor Montagu as leader and special feature writer, Lt.-Col. Hans Kahle as military correspondent. Hans Kahle's authoritative military writing was of the greatest value to the *Daily Worker* throughout the war; a former German regular officer of World War I, anti-Nazi exile and Communist leader, Hans had been a famous divisional commander in the International Brigade in Spain; he rapidly became a firm favourite of the entire staff, mechanical as well as editorial, and everyone was saddened by his untimely death a bare year after his return to Germany, where he served as police chief of the important Land of Mecklenburg in the Soviet Zone.[*]

And what of the paper whose "New Series No. 1"—actually it was numbered 3,431, following directly the issue on the day of the ban—came with such toil and sweat off the press to the cheers of the crowd that jam-packed the Caledonian Press yard by Swinton Street in the dusk of that September Sunday evening? Its spirit was unchanged but its form and content were markedly different. William Rust later summed it up in these

**Our War Babies**

" O.K., Grandpa. We're Coming !"

words: "When the paper was republished in September, 1942, there took place the decisive transformation of the *Daily Worker* from a propaganda organ into a real newspaper." For the first time the full agency services of the *Press Association* and *Reuter* (later also the *British United Press*) were taken. In place of a single main edition going in the early evening, the paper had three full editions, the final (Late London)

..................................................

* Not among the immediate newcomers, but making his bow in our issue of February 1, 1943, was the pocket cartoonist Dyad, creator of the immortal Alfie and his brother, who began their life with us as Our War Babies (above).

going at 1.15 a.m., replating when necessary later still, so that for the first time it could stand up to the other papers in news treatment. This was the salutary result of the disappearance of the long-standing wholesalers' ban in the wake of Mr. Morrison's 2D.* Under the pressure of the wartime space famine, the advertisers' boycott broke down; the girl enthusiast who was heard to say incredulously to her companion as she got her first copy: "Look! *Bourgeois* ads in *our* Daily!" was really facing a startling new fact in the paper's history; advertising revenue was very soon running at £500 a week and at its peak was to reach three times that figure.

That the situation for the revived and transformed paper was favourable beyond all precedent was seen in the orders received for the first number—no less than 550,000 copies. Unhappily the frigid strictness of the newsprint rationing authorities pegged our initial print at the paltry figure of 75,000. By technical devices, like the use of extra-light newsprint, this was shortly screwed up to 83,000, then to 96,000 (end 1943) and an absolute ceiling of 100,000-101,000 (end 1944). Our new format of six 17-in. columns fell about half-way between our old tabloid size and the standard morning newspaper size of eight 22-in. columns; but, though four pages in this format took substantially less

........................................

* Our precarious staff position was, by the way, enhanced by this. Like other daily papers printing only in London, the first edition (for Scotland and the North) had to be produced during the day, the final edition during the night. A double editorial and composing room shift was therefore necessary.

newsprint, copy for copy, than our pre-ban eight pages, to four pages we were confined. The slogan "Ten Readers for Every Copy" was prominently displayed in the early issues of the revived paper and a large "non-buying readership" was built up. It was estimated that up to half a million people every day read the *Daily Worker*.

A memorandum prepared by William Rust on the eve of republication indicated the general directive for the "decisive change" in the paper, as the following excerpts show:

"The success of the paper chiefly depends on the correct presentation of the political line of the Communist Party and the technical achievement of a very high standard of journalism. These two conditions of success are put together because they are indeed inseparable; good journalism without a correct line, or a correct line unpopularly presented, spell failure ...*

"All heavy, stereotyped political writing must be avoided. The leading articles must be written in an easy style and an elastic policy must be pursued with regard to features; no tying down to general articles on set subjects, but a quick adaptation to changing events ...

"The outstanding characteristic of the *Daily Worker*

* Throughout 1943 and 1944 William Rust gave unremitting personal attention to this dual problem—the political and technical education of the editorial staff. A series of memoranda by him as Editor touched on such themes as the cultivation of political news sense, the writing of good headlines, the raising of individual quality of work and the like.

must be its anti-Fascism; it must become the most popular anti-Fascist paper in the country and the most consistent exponent of national unity, based on working-class unity. It must become widely known because of its serious and authoritative treatment of big issues.... And although the daily exposition of policy must always be on the basis of news, this must be expressed in the form of sustained campaigns around the main issues (Second Front, production, unity, India).

"In the main the *Daily Worker* will be judged by its achievement on the industrial front.... The strongest claims have been made by the trade unions of what the *Daily Worker* will be able to do in the sphere of production. It is no exaggeration to say that the *Daily Worker* stands or falls by what it achieves in the fight for increased production; this will be the main test applied to it."

This policy was expressed in the "declaration of aims" by the Editorial Board given big play on the front page of the September 7 issue under the bold three-column headline "How to Win the War." This declaration took its stand on the main issues mentioned above, carrying forward with practical programmatic points the Board's declaration of July, 1941 (see p. 189). It was a plain, virile statement of the creed of a people's paper waging a people's war. "We shall speak," said the Board, "for the millions of ordinary folk, the men and women in industry and the Services, whose toil and courage and sacrifice will bring victory and the new world of security."

The response to the *Daily Worker's* reappearance was most imposing alike in its enthusiasm and its breadth. It was with just pride that the paper gave prominence on its front page to a facsimile of a greetings cable from the Ack-Ack gunners of George Cross Malta, to be followed three days later by airgraphed greetings from R.A.F. men training in Canada. The *Daily Mirror* hailed our first issue with a cartoon showing a newspaper winging its way from a cage, captioned "bon voyage." And that this wide response was a continuing and extending thing was spectacularly shown at an impressive conference at the Central Hall, Westminster, on February 27, 1943, when 1,169 delegates from trade union and other organisations representing a membership of over 538,000 gathered to greet the first six months of the revived *Daily Worker* and to discuss its further development. The conference agreed on important additions to the Editorial Board, notably the Dean of Canterbury,* the celebrated actress Beatrix Lehmann and three outstanding trade union leaders in the persons of Arthur Horner (miners), J.R. Scott (engineers) and A.F. Papworth (transport workers). It unanimously endorsed the report on the paper's initial fulfilment of its tasks, of which this was the principal passage:

"The central issue around which the *Daily Worker* has campaigned is the Second Front in Europe.... It came out strongly for Anglo-Soviet unity, uncompromisingly

...............................................

* Hewlett Johnson, who earned the nickname "the Red Dean" for his Christian communism.—J.E.

denounced Darlan and Darlanism,* vigorously supported the Beveridge Report, raised sharply the question of the unity of the Labour movement, declared strongly for the fighting alliance with the Indian people, and opened fire on the vested interests which are sabotaging the war effort and the people's aspirations for an enduring peace."

Indeed, the Second Front was then the issue of issues. For the *Daily Worker* reappeared as the fate of the world hung on the outcome of the Battle of Stalingrad. In that inexpressible inferno on the banks of the Volga the most awful and most decisive battle of history was being fought. And the enemies of the people were speculating on a German victory. "Stalingrad will be taken. You may be sure of that," screamed Hitler; "its capitulation seems certain," echoed Lord Kemsley's *Daily Sketch;* and in another London newspaper office this writer saw an advance proof of a feature article beginning with the words "Now that Stalingrad has fallen …"

Day after day the news from Stalingrad led all on our front page. The moment of supreme crisis in mid-September, when the Germans reached their farthest point of penetration into the warrior city, brought our leading article forward from its conventional position on p.2 to the first column of p.1, whereafter

......................................

* François Darlan, a powerful figure in the Vichy France régime who agreed with the US to switch sides on condition he became the French leader in North Africa. Darlanism was the idea that the Allies could win the war by making expedient deals with the weaker Axis powers such as Italy.—J.E.

The *Daily Worker's* report from September 16, 1942, of the "moment of supreme crisis" for the Soviet Union in the Battle of Stalingrad

it stayed; its effect was much enhanced and it could be changed at a far later hour. Buttressing the battle news we gave big play to every piece of political and military argument and agitation, every report of mass pressure, for the Second Front. The big vote of 1,500,000 at the Blackpool T.U.C. for action immediately; the unanimous resolution of the Transport and General Workers' Union Executive; the Trafalgar Square demonstration of 50,000 in October, where the speakers included John Gordon, *Sunday Express* editor, and Aneurin Bevan; the powerful "prodding" by the late Wendell Wilkie,* then touring the U.S.S.R.

......................................

\* A close friend, adviser and speechwriter for Roosevelt who served as a minister before World War II then acted as Roosevelt's emissary to both

On September 19 the accusing finger was pointed at the powers of darkness in the Cabinet, under the bold headline "These Men Must Go!" Lord Halifax, Sir Samuel Hoare (as Lord Templewood then still was; he had just told the Chelsea Tories of his fears of post-war "anarchy" against which there must be "garrisons in Europe"), L.S. Amery, Sir James Grigg, Lord Simon were named. On September 24 a blistering leader entitled "Shame" voiced the bitterness and frustration of the militant masses, a bitterness second only to that of the Munich days: "Stalingrad is ablaze with a light that fires the hearts of men…. Only from our country with its millions of men trained and armed comes no response." On November 7, while confidently telling the strained Soviet people and armies that their turn was coming ("there will be a holiday in our street"), Stalin sharply warned that "the absence of a Second Front may end badly for the Allies."

When the tide turned, as it did in November, the *Daily Worker* did not relax its efforts. The El Alamein offensive and the North Africa landings were welcomed in a four-column call by the Political Committee of the Communist Party—"fight, work and sacrifice to make the African offensive a triumphant success." As the colossal counter-offensives of the Red Army began to grind the Stalingrad Germans to dust, the paper bluntly warned against any sitting back with relief. "Let Us Rejoice—and Act" ran an apt banner line. On February 1, 1943, came the breath-

......................................................
Churchill and Stalin during the war.—J.E.

taking news of the surrender of Field-Marshal Paulus and all his remaining troops, the final disclosure of the magnitude of the German disaster, so immense that the Nazis could not hush it up, and the heart of all Germany fell into its boots.[*]

Now, surely, we cried in leader after leader, was the day and the hour to strike. American opinion was strong for action. Even the Tory Press here was shaken off the party line momentarily and called for the Second Front; "hit the enemy hard when he's groggy," urged the London *Evening News*. Lord Beaverbrook raised the question in the Lords, to be told by Lord Simon that bombing was really a Second Front (Harry Hopkins, no less, was later to explode that specious alibi). There were torrents of verbal eulogy of the Russians. Red Army day was officially celebrated on February 22 with an Albert Hall pageant, at which Mr. Anthony Eden made an impeccable speech debunking Goebbels' Bolshevik bogey.[†] But no deeds matched the words.

......................................

[*] Beatrice Webb, whose death at 85 on April 30, 1943, the *Daily Worker* was to mourn as that of "one of the country's greatest women," had reiterated her faith in Soviet Communism and had supported the Second Front in one of her last public utterances, an interview in our columns on January 27, 1943. The famous Socialist pioneer added: "Everyone must realise the predominance of Russia in winning the war, just as they must recognise she will be predominant in making the peace. I am very hopeful that Russia may—I am sure she will—justify her philosophy in the way she will handle the peace. We ourselves are bound to be puzzled, for we will not be a united nation."

[†] Some of the words of those days are still worth recording. They were words of great truth. In a massive first leader on the Red Army *The Times* wrote

To many worthy folk at the time the situation must have seemed quite puzzling. Stalin's May 1 order—it made one of our first 4 a.m. replates—put the obvious point: an immediate common blow by the Allies could turn Hitler's crisis into a catastrophe. Within a few days came the final swift victory in North Africa with the fall of Tunis and Bizerta. It was a complete debacle for the Axis, as Stalin's speedy congratulations recognised. The road to Europe lay open, as the *Daily Worker* explained in gross and in detail on May 10. But again nothing happened. And so—to borrow a phrase from a later leader—"German morale being kept going by the absence of the blow in the West," the Wehrmacht High Command was able in July, 1943, to mount its super-colossal offensive of the whole war, the monster Battle of the Kursk Salient, four times as heavy as Stalingrad.

No, the situation was not really puzzling at all. The key to it was given by Harry Pollitt when he told the Communist Party Executive in October that "the Second Front means a short war and a people's peace." Which were precisely the two things that Churchill and his fellow-reactionaries in Britain and America

..................................................

(February 22, 1943): "The people's army of the days of weakness in 1918 is still the people's at this moment of their supreme and victorious effort; it is because through these 25 years it has never lost touch with the people or ceased to draw its strength from the people's life that it has proved itself invincible by all the malice of the invader." On the same day the paper's Moscow correspondent concluded a remarkable feature with the words: "the Red Army is a thinking army, in whose minds you find the unquenchable curiosity of Russian people as you find their richness of talent and their great-heartedness."

did not want. The Moore-Brabazon "indiscretion" cited in the previous chapter had reflected all too accurately their inmost thoughts—a long war, to bleed Russia and Germany white (particularly Russia), and a peace that would guarantee their mercenary imperialist interests in Europe (by establishing those "garrisons" against "anarchy" of which Hoare had spoken).

With this in mind the *Daily Worker* did not pull its punches in dealing with the Anglo-American conferences at Casablanca (January, 1943) and Quebec (August), where the over-riding issue appeared to be the still further postponement of the Second Front. On September 1 a leader sharply put the demand for a Three-Power conference to end these delaying tactics. Despite the Allied landings in Italy, it was noted that the Germans were still moving troops to the Eastern Front (September 17). Harry Pollitt warned a great London demonstration that the Fifth Column, as evidenced by the Hearst Press in America, were playing for terms with Fascism (September 19). Shipping was now authoritatively admitted to be adequate for a European invasion (October 7). A Communist Party manifesto exposed the dangers of delay (October 19).

The high summer of 1943 had again brought us the most favourable opportunities for giving the Fascist enemy his death blow. Stalin's announcement that the Battle of the Kursk Salient had ended in the total defeat of the Germans—who had in fact shot their last major offensive bolt of the war—coincided with the sensational news of the fall of Mussolini. "Now for Hitler," was the title of the *Daily Worker's* immediate leader (July 26)—"it would be fatal to falter now and temporise with the dark forces who used Mussolini.... Now is the moment when the Axis is cracking." But the only parallel Allied action was the first of the new super-raids on German towns, the famous 2,300-tonner on Hamburg. Otherwise Mr. Churchill, in his "stew-in-their-own-juice" speech in the Commons next day, made it plain that faltering and temporising it was to be. Forty days elapsed before Allied troops landed. Marshal Badoglio, the Duce's successor, was able to surmount the tide of mass revolt of which our front page had blazoned the great news ("Great Anti-Fascist Rallies Sweep North Italy," July 28; "Milan Workers Strike for Peace," July 29). Even after the landings German paratroopers were able to rescue the detained Mussolini, who thus could do useful service for his Hitlerite masters until the last days of the war, when he met his just deserts at the hands of an Italian partisan firing squad.

There was indeed something quite queer about the Allies' Italian strategy, which Mr. Churchill made peculiarly his own. Had he not coined the phrase "the soft underbelly of Europe"? It was a sufficiently odd description of the most unfavourable terrain on the Continent for modern mobile warfare—mountainous and river-scarred. It was doubly odd when action was withheld to the point that the Germans were allowed to harden up whatever "softness" there might be. It was trebly odd that, when the blow was finally struck (in the far-off rocky south instead of the open and populous plains of the north) and the Germans were in fact taken completely by surprise and thrown into utter disarray, the speedy exploitation that could have opened up the whole south of the peninsula was deliberately checked. A precious fortnight was allowed to slip away, to the chagrin of the airborne shock troops who had brilliantly achieved the initial surprise,* the Germans gained time to rally and dig in, and the long, gruelling and costly slog "up the spine" began. "Why" asked our leader of September 16, "were the Germans permitted to seize the initiative?" There was no answer. Nor was there to our pungent description of the claim that Italy was a second front, as "bamboozling the people" (September 6).

An immediate political by-product of this campaign in Italy proved of major significance for the future. This was the entry on the scene of Amgot (Allied Military Government of Occupied Territory). The *Daily Worker* was first in the field with exposures of the activities of this organisation of American big business representatives in uniform, concerned with economic exploitation and tolerating the old Fascist local officials (September 4). A timely repudiation of Amgot's undemocratic character followed from Dame Anne Loughlin in her presidential address to the Southport T.U.C., then meeting.

All this while tremendous events were in train on the Eastern

......................................

* Fred Pateman, news editor of the *Daily Worker*, was one of the first paratroopers in at Taranto and personally confirms the total surprise of the enemy. He tells how, bright and early on a September morning, he and his comrades took their first prisoner, a German quartermaster returning from a night out in civvies, with his regimentals neatly packed in a small suitcase. The German's face, says Pateman, was a study in stunned shock.

Front, so tremendous that Stalin was shortly to speak of the "radical turn" in the whole course of the war. The German defeat at Kursk was followed by immediate Soviet counter-offensives which on August 5 simultaneously freed Orel and Bielgorod—"a victory as great as Stalingrad" (*Daily Worker,* August 6). Warfare had never before known a barrage so shattering as that put over by the Soviet guns, rockets, and dive-bombers at Orel—ten times the weight of metal fired by the Germans at Verdun in World War I. This resounding victory opened the way for the Soviet general offensive, which now began to flood through the Ukraine and the Donbas; before the end of August Kharkov and Stalino were liberated.

In this situation all eyes turned to the Trades Union Congress, meeting at Southport in September. The *Daily Worker* presented a three-column photomontage-surrounded leader, "Workers Look to the T.U.C."; since that traditional bastion of Right-wing policies, the Transport and General Workers' Union, had recently bluntly reaffirmed its 1942 resolution for the Second Front, it was expected that Congress would make an unequivocal call likewise. What actually happened was the Great Southport Hoax, which brought Sir Walter Citrine (as he still was) and the *Daily Worker* into violent conflict, for we did not hesitate to speak out savagely. The Second Front discussion was simply sidetracked by Citrine reading a news message on combined exercises in the Channel which led Congress to believe that the cross-Channel invasion had begun, brought the delegates cheering to their feet, and so to the next item on the agenda. It was an astounding incident, amply justifying what Citrine called our "diabolical attacks."

But the delaying tactics of the Churchillites and their Labour lieutenants could not stand much longer in the face of the Soviet offensive. At the end of September the enemy was whipped out of Smolensk and at the beginning of October the Dnieper, first of the great river lines which the retreating Germans might have been expected to hold for a long time, was forced. Delay now had become too dangerous for the delayers. At last there was genuine agreement on the time, place and scope of the Second Front—"only when it became clear that the Soviet Union was in a position, unaided by the Allies and with its own forces, to occupy the whole of Germany and to liberate the peoples of Europe" (*A History of the U.S.S.R.,* Vol. III, Moscow, 1948, p. 410). Agreement was reached at the historic Stalin-Roosevelt-Churchill conference at Teheran in December, 1943, preceded by the Moscow conference in November of the Foreign Ministers of the three Powers, where the general programme for international co-operation and security after the war was outlined.

The *Daily Worker* could assuredly look back with pride on the pertinacity and vigour of its Second Front campaign; equally well did it stand up to its "main test," the fight for increased production.* The hard facts of its achievement soon wrung tribute from

..............................................

* The paper's "worker correspondents," of whom a total of about 300 were functioning at this time, were invaluable as our eyes and ears in factory and workshop in relation to the production drive. From their tip-offs and rough

the Ministries concerned. In November, 1942, a shop stewards' national production week was given heavy play when the rest of the Press was strangely silent; the spirit of emulation brought recorded output increases of a sensational character. Through the following months and years production news-stories and features spotlighted the aircraft industry, shipbuilding, the great work of joint production committees, the rôle of the women engineers (at last admitted to the A.E.U.). When a serious local strike at Barrow in September, 1943, created a difficult and tense situation the *Daily Worker's* responsible handling contrasted sharply with the shameless demagogy and irresponsibility of the Tory newspapers.

Coal was a major bottleneck in war production; and the *Daily Worker* gave the inept direction of the Fuel Ministry no rest. It pioneered the demand for coal rationing, campaigned for unified control of the industry, played up every instance of pits boosting output, exposed the coalowners' inadequate "plans." From December 1942 onwards, authoritative features by Arthur Horner, and informed leaders, made a constructive contribution second to none to the solution of the wartime coal problem (e.g., "Calling All Miners," December 30, 1942; "All Hands to the Pits," August 30, 1943; "The Great Coal Scuttle," October 14, 1943). The paper fought determinedly for the miners' just demands on wages, as witnessed in its handling of the Porter

......................................................

material staff reporters were able to work up excellent and inspiring stories that no other newspaper got.

award and the miners' wage movement of January-April, 1944. In
sum, the achievement of the *Daily Worker* and the Communist
Party in the coalfields at this period was appropriately characterised in the phrase of miners' president Will Lawther—"the
Redder the pit the greater the output."

Next major issue was that of the unity of the Labour movement. In 1943 the Communist Party launched a new campaign
for its affiliation to the Labour Party; and of this campaign the
*Daily Worker* was the most effective weapon. Our pages reflected
and directed the movement for affiliation which secured the
support of over 3,000 working-class bodies. The dissolution of
the Communist International in May was thought by many
to have destroyed the Labour Party Executive's last argument
against affiliation; but, true to form, that body hardened its
heart and at the Party conference in London at Whitsun, Mr.
Morrison secured the rejection of affiliation by 1,951,000 votes
to 712,000. It was, nevertheless, the largest pro-affiliation vote
ever recorded, amounting to over a quarter of the conference.
And it did not accurately reflect the trends in union opinion;
thus the N.U.R. annual general meeting did not meet till after
the conference, when it voted in favour of affiliation.

This rejection of Communist affiliation was far from ending
the unity campaign so far as the *Daily Worker* was concerned.
Leading members of the Labour Party, like Professor Laski and
Mr. Shinwell,* expressed their views in our columns on the need

...................................................

* Manny Shinwell, who emerged from Red Clydeside to become chairman

for talks between the Labour Party and the Communist Party with a view to securing Labour and progressive unity to defeat the Tories at the General Election. Shinwell spoke acidly of some of his colleagues' "veneration for musty and cobwebbed arguments which obscure the real issue." In April, 1944, the *Daily Worker* called a unity conference in London which secured wide representation of working-class and progressive opinion, with 1,762 delegates representing over 2,000,000 people; the conference endorsed an appeal by the A.E.U. Executive Council to the Labour Party to call a general conference to formulate a common working-class electoral policy. The same view was later expressed by 131 Executive members of unions affiliated to the Labour Party.

The spirit of unity was strong in the trade union movement, too. This was naturally a source of particular satisfaction to the *Daily Worker,* since by its reporting of union activities of every kind—from congress to branch resolutions—and its featuring of union problems and interests, it had made itself the trade unionists' own newspaper. The anti-Communist "Black Circular'" was finally quashed by the Southport T.U.C. in 1943. At Blackpool in 1944, A.F. Papworth was the first Communist to be elected to the General Council, thus symbolising the new militant leader-

---

of the Labour Party and, after the war, the Minister of Fuel and Power responsible for nationalising the coal industry.—J.E.

\* A document banning Communists from holding union office. See p.255.—J.E.

ship that was emerging at national level in the unions. On the world front the initial moves by the British T.U.C. for a new all-in union body were warmly welcomed by the *Daily Worker* (October 28, 1943), which later gave the widest coverage to the eleven-day world congress of unions in London in February, 1945, where the basis of the World Federation of Trade Unions was laid. On the home front the remarkable General Council post-war reconstruction report, hailed as a programme for a planned economy and full employment that could command united support, was put over in an imposing whole-page feature (October 3, 1944). Central conception of the programme was the public control over, and democratisation of, the whole of Britain's economic life.

Sir William Beveridge (as he then was) had been consulted by the T.U.C. General Council in the drafting of their programme. His historic social security plan was still the talk of the country. From the first publication of the Beveridge Plan in December, 1942, the *Daily Worker* gave it wide space and development, featuring readers' letters and an exclusive series of answers by Beveridge himself to questions propounded by the paper, rebutting attacks (by the Kemsley newspapers, for example), subjecting the Government's subsequent "Beveridge-and-Water" employment and social security schemes to detailed and searching criticism.

Even to summarise the paper's constant references during this period to the general problems of post-war reconstruction, and the specific problems of education, health, the land and planning, would require a chapter. It must suffice to cite its exceptional record on that question of questions—housing. A leader in July, 1943, forcefully raised the whole matter and thereafter housing was top priority for *Daily Worker* home news and features. In the autumn of 1944 a planned editorial campaign, dealing both with the blitz repairs scandal* in London and with housing in general, rated no fewer than 150 stories, with leaders and features which put the demand for a Minister of Housing to tackle seriously the super-acute problem.

Next to its leading campaign for the Second Front the *Daily Worker* fought perhaps its keenest political battles in carrying out the behest to make itself the pre-eminent and most consistent anti-Fascist paper. For this involved the whole question of the nature of the liberation of Europe's enslaved peoples from Fascism. Was it to be a genuine liberation for the democratic masses of the Continent or merely the substitution of Lord Templewood's Anglo-American "garrisons against anarchy," with the assistance of local reactionary forces, for the iron heel of German Fascism? Alone in the British Press, the *Daily Worker* fought throughout on the side of the mass movements of national liberation, which embraced the entire progressive forces of their respective countries,

..................................................

* By 1944 damage from the blitz and the new flying bombs had caused a massive housing shortage in London—the East End borough of Poplar alone lost 8,500 houses. The government was widely criticised for its failure to carry out repairs or provide temporary homes in the face of an overcrowding crisis which, it was feared, would get much worse when demobbed soldiers and evacuated families began returning home in 1945.—J.E.

and of which the organised working class led by heroic and unwavering Communist Parties formed the core. The Anglo-American reactionaries, particularly Churchill, stuck to the Templewood line, except when relentlessly winkled out of it.

France was the first cockpit of this particular struggle. And a severe shock was administered to the democratic world when the Allies, on landing in North Africa, sought to do a deal with the Vichyite and collaborator Admiral Darlan, around whom gathered creatures of a comparable kidney like MM. Flandin, Pucheu (later executed as a traitor) and Peyrouton. Darlan's assassination nonplussed the Darlanites in high places in London and Washington, but they sought every opportunity thereafter to intrigue against the bona fide Committee of National Liberation. The *Daily Worker* kept an unwavering spotlight on these murky moves. When Fernand Grenier, French Communist leader, escaped to London in January, 1943, and told the first full and inspiring story of the magnificent fight of the French Resistance, we gave that story everything we had. In July, 1943, Frank Pitcairn was sent—more than a little adventurously—to Algiers and returned with a striking series "Where France Begins." We fought against the policy which starved the French Resistance of arms, to be justified by the tribute which General Eisenhower paid in June, 1944, to the invaluable military assistance of the Resistance warriors. It was with pride as well as in solidarity that we could salute the eventual liberation of Paris—by the superb rising of the Parisians themselves—with the glowing banner "City of Liberty and Glory."

Yugoslavia was the next test case; and here an "old gang" Government in exile purported to control a resistance movement led on the spot by its War Minister, General Mihailovich. Beginning with a leader and a big feature on December 21, 1942, the *Daily Worker* was able to show that this was a myth. Mihailovich was not resisting the Germans but was in fact aiding them by using his "chetniks" to fight the genuine People's Army of Liberation. The facts which the *Daily Worker* persistently pressed were borne out by the Allied military missions parachuted to both sides. In December, 1943, the Liberation Army was officially recognised as an allied force, and in August, 1944, a reconstructed Yugoslav Government finally repudiated the traitorous Mihailovich. We were certainly justified in the headline "Truth Wins," which we placed over our editorial comment that day.

Poland's case was a deal graver. There was a large Polish military and political emigration in this country, headed by a Government financed and favoured in every way by the British Government. Reactionary, anti-Soviet and even pro-Fascist, these dubious characters disposed of a preposterous Press apparatus out of all proportion in a period of acute paper shortage; the *Daily Worker* was able to give detailed facts about the ownership and character of 33 newspapers and journals—and they were not all. In April, 1943, these Polish gentry opened a vicious attack on the Soviet Union on the basis of Goebbels' propaganda about a mass grave of Polish officers "shot by the Russians" discovered at Katyn (evidence was soon forthcoming, as might be expected, that it was a massacre by the Germans). While reiterating, through the mouth of Stalin himself, its desire to see a strong and independent Poland, the U.S.S.R. was compelled to break off relations with the London Poles.

Through all the complicated diplomatic and political exchanges that followed the *Daily Worker* set itself the double task of enlightenment and exposure, which culminated in the tragedy of the Warsaw rising of August-September, 1944. The British Press fell completely for what was a monstrous provocation by the London Poles and their local military chief, General Bor-Komarowski, aiming to offset the establishment of a patriotic Government on liberated Polish territory (at Lublin) with a Polish Army fighting side by side with the Russians. An anti-Soviet tone grew with the propounding of questions about the alleged refusal of Russian aid to Warsaw, or the refusal of the Russians to allow Allied planes to drop arms and munitions to the insurgents. Only the *Daily Worker* printed the news that Bor had refused Soviet aid; only the *Daily Worker* (and *The Times*) printed the vital statement by Lublin's General Zymierski that arms dropped over Warsaw must, because of the dispersed nature of the rising, fall into the hands of the Germans. Rightly we kept our heads and gave our readers the full facts of the Polish crisis—"the test of the future of Europe" (September 12, 1944). The Yalta agreement of the Big Three proved that we were correct.

As the vision of victory began to take shape encouragement of the dark forces abroad was paralleled at home. The perpetrators of the disgusting desecration of the Lenin Memorial in

The *Daily Worker* goes "right over the top" on November 18, 1943, in response to the news of Oswald Mosley's impending release

Holford Square, Finsbury, were never brought to book. And in November, 1943, the country was outraged by the release from 18B internment of Mosley. The *Daily Worker* was able to warn of this a week before it took place and went right over the top with an after-midnight splash and leader when it was officially announced. The popular and Labour movement reaction was one of the most indignant and universal ever known. Mr. Morrison's "blunder" was castigated by the National Council of Labour itself and protests poured into our office at the rate of one a minute on the peak day (November 19). Mass lobbying of the House of Commons—with banners reading "Cage Mosley! Rats Spread Disease!"—was on an impressive scale. Herbert, sneering at "mob hysteria," was only saved by the then Tory majority, to the tune of 327 to 62. The *Daily Worker,* which had even secured a vitriolic feature from the not-too-friendly H.G. Wells, could take pride in its voicing of the national anger at this scandal.

At this point we may well note how those who were discovering such tenderness for Hitler's friends here continued to hamper the *Daily Worker* just as much as they possibly could.

**ALL THERE—BAR DAILY WORKER**

ALL newspapers—with the exception of the *Daily Worker*—have begun to print the reports of their Second Front war correspondents.

As the operations develop reports from these correspondents will flow 'in. Only the *Daily Worker* is prevented from serving its readers and the country in this way.

This War Office ban has been widely condemned throughout the country as a violation of the freedom of the Press.

The *Daily Worker* is now renewing it efforts to secure the appointment of a correspondent.

The *Daily Worker's* D-Day reports of June 7, 1944, lament the lack of a war correspondent

It was not until August, 1943, that an impudent ban on the export of the paper was removed, after strong trade union protests. More serious was the refusal to allow the paper a war correspondent. We only asked for one, when the *Daily Express* had 22, the *News Chronicle* 11, and so on; but the Cabinet said "No"— on the insolent, and absurd, "political" grounds that Communists could not be trusted with secret information. William Rust later disclosed that Mr. Churchill himself was mainly responsible for this ban, as part of his general Communist-phobia, and did not really believe that Communists were unreliable—he thought the accusation would be a good way of besmirching them. Against this disgraceful discrimination the paper developed a campaign second only to the campaign against the ban itself.

Trade union protests climaxed in the passing of a unanimous protest resolution by the Blackpool T.U.C. in 1944. M.P.s of all parties signed a petition to the Government. But it was not till Mr. Churchill had fallen that this last of the bans was removed, in September, 1945.[*]

The glorious Sixth of June, 1944, opened up the last triumphant lap of the war. The *Daily Worker* rode the news whirlwind of those days with credit. Many were the quick changes, the late replates, the new leaders, the re-made front pages, as on the sensational night of July 21 when the attempted assassination of Hitler showed that Nazism was near its death throes. From D-Day onwards our leader was brought down across the foot of the front page, so as to give the maximum top display for the war news (and there it was to stay until we left Swinton Street). Soon we had the additional complication of constant enemy fire, as London fought its way through the 80 days' battle of the Vls; but despite the crescendo roar of the approaching flying bomb—and the still more sinister cut-off—despite the constant flashing of the roof-spotter's "imminent danger" red light, not an edition was missed. Then came the V2s, the faster-than-sound

........................................

[*] How the war correspondent ban was turned into a positive persecution was seen in the case of Clemens Dutt, who went to Algiers as our special correspondent in December 1943, was accepted by the French military authorities as a war correspondent and duly took part in the invasion of the South of France in August 1944. Within a couple of days the British War Office arbitrarily intervened and compelled the French authorities to withdraw him.

rockets. In common with all national newspapers, we officially (but secretly) knew that it was touch-and-go whether these blackguardly weapons might not make London untenable; and we shared in the common plans for newspaper evacuation. Our refuge, all arranged down to a hostel for the staff, was to be in the antique plant of a small evening paper at Nuneaton.

As the avengers pressed on into Germany from West and East, as the Soviet offensive knocked out one Hitler satellite after another and the thunder of Russian guns was heard in Berlin, the unity of the Big Three was consummated at the Yalta conference of Roosevelt, Stalin and Churchill. On February 13, 1945, ten columns of the *Daily Worker* were devoted to the "great tidings"—the agreement on the United Nations and continuing co-operation in peace, on the Polish question, etc. A week later we were able to expose the machinations of a group of diehards who sought "under the hat" (as they put it) to organise opposition to Yalta; they were overwhelmed in the Commons debate, after Eden had warned them to "take care you do not fall victims to the Nazis' anti-Soviet wiles."

(Above and opposite) How the story of the attempted assassination of
Hitler developed across four editions, including a rare 4 a.m. special

Identical views upon the future came in those days from both
West and East. Churchill said: "the future of the world depends
upon the united action in the next few years … of the three most
powerful Allies. If that fails, all fails; if that succeeds a broad
future for all nations may be assured," Stalin said that the Great
Alliance "is founded not on casual, transitory considerations,
but on vital and lasting interests"; actions by the United Nations
to end any threat of war "will be effective if the Great Powers
which have borne the brunt of the war against Hitler Germany
continue to act in a spirit of unanimity and accord. They will
not be effective if this essential condition is violated." Headed
"Britain and Russia," a *Daily Worker* leader on the earlier Stalin-
Churchill talks in Moscow rammed the point home:

   "Fundamental conflicts … will now be excluded for all
   time, providing the British people succeed in preventing
   the rise to power and influence of those in our midst who
   hate the Soviet Union and its Socialist achievement more
   than they love Britain. This warning is given with deep

seriousness. As victory approaches the fight against reaction at home will become more and more the fundamental issue before the British people.... If the democratic Powers were to fall out humanity would again be threatened by the revival of aggression and a terrible new war." (November 8, 1944.)

Yet when victory, the most overwhelming military victory in all history, was consummated in April-May, 1945, there was shadow as well as sunshine in the prospect. Even while the bestial face of Fascism had been irrevocably unmasked with the over-running of the appalling death camps of Belsen and Buchenwald, the Hitlerites continued their disruptive game. And, though Field-Marshal Montgomery rightly rebuffed the impudent attempt to surrender to the Western Allies only, there was a strange tolerance of Admiral Doenitz, Hitler's "successor," an unnatural affability towards Goering and other surrendered war criminals, which caused us sharply to denounce "The New Plot." Had we not previously warned that "the danger is that powerful reactionary influences will protect the war criminals, the Junkers and the big industrialists, and will favour a 'soft' peace with the ultimate objective of using a revived Germany as a counterpoise to the Soviet Union" (leader, November 11, 1944)?

But the deepest shadow had already fallen over the other end of Europe. The betrayal of liberation in Greece, for which Mr. Churchill above all must bear the historic responsibility, was to present the *Daily Worker* with a cause and a campaign only paralleled in its history by the war in Spain. The thing started with the desire to disarm the patriot partisans once the country was liberated from the Germans. This was a general feature of "Western" liberation; in November, 1944, it caused a considerable crisis in France, and even more in Belgium, where General Erskine, the British G.O.C., intervened openly on the side of the reactionary Pierlot Government against the resistance men. In Greece the situation was complicated by the fact that the entire country outside Athens was in the hands of the Communist-led united resistance movement (E.A.M.) and its armed forces (E.L.A.S.), that the corrupt and Fascist Greek ruling class had been the most nakedly collaborationist in Europe, and that it was proposed to maintain Royalist-Fascist special formations under arms. *The Times* special correspondent in Athens (December 11, 1944) gave the political essence of the situation when he described the—

> "general distrust on the part of the Greek masses of a Government which had not carried out any of the 'house cleaning' which seemed so necessary to a people who had suffered not only occupation but previous dictatorship.... Right-wing extremists were definitely fomenting discord.... The British attitude is influenced by those of the Right wing, previously collaborators, who rushed to the British when they entered Greece, offered their services, and in many instances had been taken on as advisers, etc."

The detailed story cannot be related here. But Churchill launched General Scobie and the British troops in Athens into full-scale war with E.L.A.S., was forced by public protest here to indicate (through Mr. Eden) terms of settlement every one of which was perfidiously flouted afterwards, and finally—with the aid of the British Ambassador, Sir Rex Leeper—put over a foul smokescreen about alleged E.L.A.S. atrocities, "hideous massacre," and the like, under cover of which the Greek Fascists could butcher their way into power, in the persons of the dug-out dictator General Plastiras and the still worse Admiral Voulgaris.[*]

The words of a *Daily Worker* telegram from Athens (March 28, 1945) were all too prophetic: "if the E.A.M. proposals for a representative Government and an Inter-Allied commission are rejected, Greece will fall definitely under Fascist-quisling rule."

Prophetic, too, for the peace to come was our general summary in a leader on January 31, 1945:

"The roots of Fascism are to be traced to the unbridled power wielded by the privileged few whose financial might enables them to ride roughshod over the democratic aspirations of the people. The fall of Hitler will not automatically

....................................................

* The *Daily Worker* devoted great attention to the battle for democracy in the Greek trade union movement, in which the British T.U.C. played a large part. Citrine visited Athens in February 1945 in this connection, but made no contacts with E.A.M. and lent himself to the Churchill propaganda over "atrocities" (*Daily Worker,* February 9, 1945). When A.F. Papworth visited Greece with a T.U.C. delegation in May he returned with a very different story of the fearful luxury-poverty contrast, of police brutality, etc. (*Daily Worker,* May 13, 1945).

destroy those roots, will not wipe out the foul teachings which have destroyed all moral standards in the minds of those who have imbibed them, will not mark the end of the quislings and Fifth Columnists who are trying to crawl back into power in the liberated countries. The fight against Fascism must be continued into the peace, continued until the rule of the people becomes unassailable in all lands. And in this mighty and creative task all men and women of good will must play their full part."

As with Fascism, so with war. Subsequent events were to give most deadly point to the leader of April 13, 1945, which, mourning the tragic and sudden death of President Roosevelt, asked "will the loss of the great leader encourage the dark forces of reaction to renew their attempts at disruption?" And following that came the words of the speech upon which the greatest American of our time was working when he was struck down. They may fittingly end this chapter: "More than an end to war we want an end to the beginning of all wars," Roosevelt wrote. "Today we are faced with the pre-eminent fact that if civilisation is to survive we must cultivate the science of human relationships—the ability of all peoples of all kinds to live together and to work together in the same world at peace.... We must go on and do all in our power to conquer the doubts, fears, ignorance and greed which made this horror possible."

## Chapter Ten

# The Only Daily Paper
# Owned by its Readers

THE POST-WAR WORLD into which the *Daily Worker* rode on the crest of the great wave of victory was to hold many disillusionments, difficulties and dangers; yet just there lay the very opportunity for us to develop into a first-class national newspaper with a mass circulation. The decisive political and journalistic turn to a popular mass paper had been made, as the previous chapter has shown, when the ban was lifted in 1942. But the technical restrictions of a small plant never intended for daily newspaper production, and the rigid rationing of newsprint, made impossible the full exploitation of that decisive turn, which had brought so substantial an increase in the paper's influence and standing. Thus when the *Daily Worker's* experts first began to sketch out post-war plans, as early as the summer of 1943, they were compelled to keep two over-riding factors constantly in mind—a new and suitable plant (both building and machinery) and free newsprint.

Our post-war planners had every sort of headache. The search for a suitable building in the blitz-devastated centre of London reduced the stoutest hearts to something near despair. To tell the whole tale of the buildings that were discovered and inspected in vain—they were too small, or too dear, or impossibly sited—would require a chapter all on its own. By the spring of 1945 there had, however, been three major disappointments; first the once-noted building of the defunct *Daily Chronicle* in Salisbury Square off Fleet Street, second an empty works in Aldgate, third a warehouse the other side of London Bridge station. And the situation was now critical. Eighteen months before the paper had been the first in the country to secure a licence for the manufacture of a new rotary press; the fact was proudly publicised in a front-page announcement by the Editorial Board in the issue of January 1, 1944; and the giant machine was being duly built in the Goss-Foster works at Preston. Was there to be no machine-room ready for its complex erection when completed?

At this moment, luckily, the building-seekers came across a stout late Victorian warehouse in Farringdon Road, of which its brush-making owners wished to dispose immediately. The site was far more convenient than we had been daring to hope—only a stone's throw from Fleet Street—and the building had deep basements. After the necessary negotiations and survey the freehold was finally acquired for £48,000 in the autumn of 1945. So at last we had our new home; though very much remained to be done to make it habitable as a daily newspaper office and plant. But before that story comes to be told our steps must be retraced to the victory month of May and the great change in the organisation of the *Daily Worker* which then first took public shape.

Hot on the heels of VE-Day, on May 12, the Shoreditch Town Hall was packed to the doors with one of the greatest and most enthusiastic of all *Daily Worker* conferences. From 12 national trade union executives, from 27 district committees, from 35 Trades Councils, from scores upon scores of union branches, shop stewards' committees and factories came the 500 delegates representing nearly 1,900,000 organised workers. The cream of the working-class movement had gathered to endorse the post-war plans of "our paper," of which No. 1 had already been indicated by the Editorial Board as "development into a front rank national newspaper with a circulation of 500,000 copies daily."

Typical of the broad character of the conference was a friendly and constructive message it received from Mr. J.B. Priestley. Underlining Mr. Priestley's points William Rust told the delegates:

"We want a paper that in size, in improved technique, in popular content and appeal, in its features, its news stories, its sport presentation, its woman interest, and in its art of writing (which is one of the key questions before our editorial staff; whether it is an article or a short report everything must be written to a high standard)—that in all these things will compete with and go one better than the millionaire Press of this country."

Rust stressed the need for a special concession of extra newsprint to the *Daily Worker,* since the pre-war percentage basis for rationing put the paper at an inequitable disadvantage as against its competitors, and would render the planned expansion impossible. He then turned to the main proposition—the launching of a co-operative society to own and publish the paper. Only so could there be a permanent guarantee of that "readers' ownership and control which is the distinguishing feature of our Press." Only so could expansion be financed, by individuals and working-class bodies, with the emergence of any dominating financial interest barred by the £200 legal limit on shareholding. The conference adopted the proposal with acclamation.

Duly registered under the Industrial and Provident Societies Acts, the People's Press Printing Society Ltd. was launched on September 12 in a *Daily Worker* front-page splash of the heaviest calibre. David Ainley, well known in the Manchester Labour movement, an experienced trade unionist and co-operative committeeman, was appointed Secretary. Application was made for affiliation to the Co-operative Union; and though this was rejected on the unconvincing ground that the P.P.P.S. might be in competition with the Co-operative Press Ltd. (if the latter ever attained its traditional ideal of publishing a daily as well as a Sunday paper), support for the application was forthcoming from a considerable number of societies. Shareholders began to flood in, one of the earliest—for the £200 maximum—being the patriarch of English letters, none other than George Bernard Shaw. In its first six months the Society reached a membership of 14,513, of which 426 were organisations (266 trade union, 45 co-operative); it had raised over £100,000 of the initial capital aims of £150,000—£95,000 in share capital—while from the Fighting Fund trustees it received non-interest bearing loan capital totalling £56,000.

The paper's sixteenth birthday celebrations were made the occasion for its ceremonial transfer to co-operative ownership. On January 6, 1946, the Albert Hall was the scene of the most imposing and elaborate function in our history—a brilliant and colourful festival and pageant with massed choirs, marching delegates, banners and fanfares, spotlighting the past, present and future of the people's paper. "Grand and gay," ran our report, "it was the paper's Festival, and it became at the same time a great Festival of the Common Man." London busmen's leader Bill Jones handed over the formal document of transfer to William Rust amid a scene of electrifying enthusiasm; and so the imprint "Printed and published by the People's Press Printing Society Ltd." marched into newspaper history. Behind that mighty enthusiasm lay two impressive social facts, which a commercial Press readership survey had just disclosed; the first was that the *Daily Worker* was the paper of the organised workers (69 per cent. of our readers were trade unionists, the highest of any paper, the next highest being the *Daily Herald,* at 45 per cent.), the second that it had a younger readership than any other paper—two-thirds of our total being in the 21-49 age groups.

These signs of change and growth in the paper's organisation paralleled the momentous changes that Victory Year brought to Britain and the world. The Tories' attempt to repeat 1918 with a snap "Khaki Election" recoiled fearfully on their heads. It was noteworthy that the Labour Party conference in May which accepted the Churchill challenge registered the closest vote ever known in favour of progressive unity (including the Communists). Mr. Jack Tanner, the engineers' president since turned witch-hunter, moved against the Executive who only managed to scrape through by 1,314,000 votes to 1,219,000. In that spirit of fighting unity Labour's troops, with the *Daily Worker* and the Communist Party in the van, battled through to victory. The Tories and their Press cut the sorriest of figures, the *Daily Express* repeating its 1939 "there will be no war this year" gaffe with bombastic prophecies of a Tory majority of 100. Above all it was the men who won the war who rejected the Man Who Won the War; the Services' vote against the Tories was overwhelming; it was a soldier who gave the *Daily Worker* its eve-of-poll slogan "Vote as Red as You Can."

On declaration day (July 26) the teleprinters were soon chattering out sensational news of Labour victories in the most unexpected spots. The Tories were engulfed in a new 1906 and for the first time the Labour Party came to power with an absolute majority, gaining 390 seats to the Tory 211, Liberals and Independents only rating 10 each. Communist representation rose to 2, Phil Piratin (Mile End) joining William Gallacher, who increased his majority in West Fife from 593 to 2,056. No less than 26 Tory ministers were defeated, five of them members of Mr. Churchill's "caretaker" Cabinet, and including such notorious reactionaries as L.S. Amery and Sir James Grigg.

In his first words as Premier-elect, that evening, Mr. Attlee said: "We are facing a new era ... we are on the eve of a great advance of the human race. That will mean not only the work which must be done here in reconstruction, but above all co-operation with other nations and particularly with our great Allies the United States of America and the U.S.S.R."

Alas! Those were soon to prove words only. The appointment of Ernest Bevin to the key post of Foreign Secretary was ominous. In a very short time Bevin made it plain that he stood for the "continuity" of foreign policy every whit as much as MacDonald had done twenty years before; and the heart of Tory foreign policy had already been disclosed by Churchill in his victory broadcast on May 13—kowtow to the Americans, cold-shoulder the Russians, fear and fight against the new popular movements that were everywhere arising against the bankrupt old order. It was noticeable that Mr. Bevin's first major utterance as Foreign Secretary, on the historic Potsdam agreement of the Big Four on Germany, failed to present that keystone of the rebuilding of a peaceful and democratic Germany—the central problem for Europe—in any positive way, and to that extent already lined up with the reactionary circles who greeted Potsdam with howls of rage.

True, Mr. Attlee greeted with enthusiasm the Soviet Union's entry into the war against Japan (August 9); but the blinding flash of the American atomic bombs on Hiroshima and Nagasaki obscured the instant and immense military achievement of the Russian Manchurian campaign, and the consequent capitulation of Japan, and seemed to send most British and American statesmen clean out of their senses. There were delighted cries that the U.S.S.R. had been "turned into a second-class Power overnight." Bevin took the earliest opportunity to roar out that Russia was "coming across the throat of the British Empire" and played a principal part in bringing to nought the London Council of Foreign Ministers in October. Talk about a "West bloc" started up. Churchill emerged as the arch-propagator of the great atomic bomb myth.*

In the midst of all this pother the *Daily Worker* kept its head. Articles by Professor Haldane and other experts soberly estimated the vast potentialities of atomic fission as an immense step forward in man's mastery of nature while urging the public international control of so appalling a weapon. And the first attempt to over-play atomic bomb diplomacy failed. In the November elections in France the Communist Party emerged as the biggest single party; some Foreign Ministers got together again in Moscow and achieved some measure of agreement for the United Nations General Assembly; the U.S.S.R. embarked confidently on its first post-war Five Year Plan.

There were certainly other problems and danger-spots in plenty. In November the opening of the Anglo-Dutch colonial

........................................

* On August 17 Churchill told the House of Commons: "It is to this atomic bomb more than to any other factor that we may ascribe the sudden and speedy ending of the war against Japan." The previous day *The Times* had written editorially "already the governing classes, headed by the Emperor, are desperately trying to 'save their face' by ascribing defeat to the atomic bomb, conveniently forgetting their request to Russia to mediate with the Allies before the atomic bomb was used …" while in the same issue a correspondent said bluntly "the assertion that new American bombs have brought the Japanese war to a magic end is a myth."

war against the new-born Indonesian Republic was a portent. After a brief period of alarm and despondency following the Labour victory, the Greek Fascists and ex-quislings took heart when they discovered that the more Mr. Bevin changed the more he was the same as Mr. Churchill; a régime of naked terror—graphically exposed by Malcolm MacEwen as our special correspondent—perpetrated preposterous "elections" and a "plebiscite" to bring back the discredited George II, and plunged unhappy Hellas into the abyss of economic ruin, murderous repression and civil war. In general, as William Rust wrote in his New Year survey (*Daily Worker,* January 1, 1946), there was a "revival of Fascist activity in numerous countries, including Britain, where Mosley and his thugs have reappeared…. Our anti-Fascist tasks have not yet ended."

That Rust article was highly prophetic. It proclaimed that 1946 would be a "testing year" for the new Labour Government whose motto must be "faster and bolder." Workers' needs must come first, with low-rented houses as priority No. 1; working-class unity was more necessary than ever. It continued:

"The good things of life are rooted in prosperous industry, and the success of Labour's social programme is dependent on the unbending carrying through of its nationalisation proposals and the breaking of the power of the vested interests. Nationalisation will not bring about magical changes: every step forward will have to be fought for, planned for and worked for … The coming year should, however, bring positive results, providing steel as well as mining comes under State ownership and providing the country is not saddled with new burdens in the shape of fantastically high rates of compensation to idle employers and redundant bankers ...

"Against Labour's programme the Tories intend to wage a ding-dong battle. It is true that the Tory Party today is ... demoralised by its electoral defeat and taking very badly to the task of Parliamentary opposition. But it would be a sorry mistake to write the Tories off. Has not Churchill foretold that 'in the next few years we shall come to fundamental quarrels in this country'? This cunning, canting crowd are biding their time. They will strike when they see a chance to turn the clock back."

'Forty-six was a testing year for the *Daily Worker,* too. The membership of the P.P.P.S. rose to 20,000. In July building work began at Farringdon Road and May 1, 1947, was widely publicised as the date for the appearance of the new *Daily Worker.* Rapidly rising costs of building and plant, however, necessitated the launching of a campaign for an extra £70,000 to bring the Society's capital resources up to a quarter of a million. In September came the first relaxation of newsprint restrictions; from the 23$^{rd}$ of that month the paper rose to six pages every day, doubling its feature space and presenting a whole page of sport, and a drive for 50,000 new readers was taken up with enthusiasm by Communist Party organisations all over the country; by the winter over 23,000 had thus been added to the daily circulation, some 16,500 of that total being in the London area. Newspaper advertising space was still at a premium and the *Daily Worker's* advertisement income reached its peak of £1,500 a week.

Demobilisation greatly strengthened the editorial staff, the return of Fred Pateman (later news editor) and W.G. Shepherd (chief sub-editor) being specially noteworthy; at the same time the paper gained its outstanding new recruit in Derek Kartun, who after a period as Paris correspondent became foreign editor. It was of this stage in our history that the *Newspaper World,* leading trade weekly, wrote:

> "Many newspapers in this country could learn some-
> thing from the exceedingly well-produced *Daily Worker.* I
> find the *Worker's* make-up an exceptional combination of
> brightness, sobriety and readability. The front-page leader
> is particularly well presented. The *Worker* is a newspaper
> with a mission; and no one can complain that it does not
> carry out that mission to the best technical advantage."

Late in the autumn of 1946 there was an unexpected develop-
ment at Farringdon Road, at first a snag though ultimately an incalculable advantage. When the preliminary work of clearing and preparing had been done the surveyors of the war damage authorities conducted their final examination and in effect condemned the entire structure above first-floor level. This meant a radical change in our plans; and, in practice, the erection of a modern steel-framed building. This made big extra demands both in expense (though a substantial contribution, some £14,000, was made by the war damage authorities) and in time required; but in the end it was to give us a first-class

modern building instead of a reconditioned old one—and with two whole extra floors, thus enabling the entire organisation to be housed under one roof with space to spare, which would not have been possible under the original plan. At the turn of 1946-47, however, all these imposing additions to the technical convenience and commercial value of Farringdon Road were not yet clearly seen; we entered that winter rather apprehensive of our May 1 deadline and conscious of a new mountain of difficulties in a time of acute shortages in both building materials and labour. We would have been something more than apprehensive if we had known what lay immediately ahead.

As for the Labour Government, it passed the test of 1946 with no credit to itself at all. The year, politically and economically, was one of rude awakening from the Utopia-round-the-corner idyll of the first months after the General Election. There was an idyllic hangover at the Labour Party Whitsun conference, the first since the election victory; amid the cheering, and in a cocksure "alone-we-did-it" spirit, Communist Party affiliation was unceremoniously rejected. But thereafter cold, remorseless reality obtruded itself more and more. Large social reforms were initiated, like the National Health and National Insurance schemes. Nationalisation began with the mines, inevitably, with transport and the utilities following later; compensation was substantial in every case and an elaborate, bureaucratic ("jobs for the boys") administrative apparatus set up; but the Government retreated precipitately from a showdown with the steel barons and that most vital of all sectors was left untouched till the introduction of the highly diluted nationalisation Bill in 1949.

There were big words about housing ("a military operation") but deeds so minor that squatting became a national phenomenon; indeed, the London squatters' movement of September was a major political event, giving us our main news story for weeks. At the Brighton Trades Union Congress the Prime Minister launched the first of many waspish attacks on Communists—the growth of the Party's influence in the trade unions had just been typified in the election of Arthur Horner to the secretaryship of the National Union of Mineworkers—and Sir Stafford Cripps in October uttered the sneer: "there is not as yet a very large number of workers in Britain capable of taking over large enterprises" (or, as the Tories used to say somewhat more succinctly, "Labour is not fit to govern").

Over all this hung the menace of the American orientation. Already the summary ending of Lend-Lease and the floating of the American loan had substituted the principles of money-lending for those of mutuality; but by the summer of 1946 the loan was prematurely exhausted as a result of the cynical cancellation of controls in the United States and the consequent skyrocketing of prices. The immediate and sensational consequence was the introduction of bread rationing in July, a grim illustration of the precarious economic position of the country.

But our rulers, old and new, showed no signs of striking out for independence; on the contrary, they clung ever more desperately to Wall Street's cross of gold, offering themselves ever more assiduously as the principal European fuglemen of the

American finance oligarchy's anti-Communist crusade for world domination. It was to Fulton, Missouri, that Mr. Churchill went as President Truman's guest to utter his notorious anti-Soviet jeremiad.* In the tense situations that developed in the United Nations Mr. Bevin automatically lined up with the American spokesmen against Mr. Molotov. Finally, on December 2, the *Daily Worker* caused a mighty stir by the exclusive disclosure of an Anglo-American military pact, providing for standardisation and co-ordination of armaments, co-operation of commands, etc. There was a hasty denial by the War Office, but the following month the whole sinister step was officially announced.

Other events of great moment were afoot in the world, however. The year was a red-letter one for *Daily Worker* special correspondents. First Ivor Montagu and then Walter Holmes covered the Nuremberg trials of the Nazi leaders, that monumental international judicial process which exposed for all time the nature of Fascism and its begetting of World War II. Betty Bartlett, the Yorkshire girl who married heroic Greek seamen's union leader Tony Ambatielos,† was a lone voice of truth over

........................................

* The "Iron Curtain" speech.—J.E.

† Ambatielos, the general secretary of the Federation of Greek Maritime Unions, had met Bartlett during World War II in Cardiff, where his federation was organising resistance to the Nazi occupation of Greece. He was arrested in Greece, along with thousands of other Communists, during the country's civil war and sentenced to death, but this was commuted to life imprisonment after an international campaign led by Bartlett. He was finally freed—and reunited with his wife in Britain—in 1968.—J.E.

the wire from Athens. R. Palme Dutt went to India as the Cripps Mission sought to save the sub-continent from its rising mass movement by a final deal with the native bourgeoisie. William Rust reported on the elections in Czechoslovakia from which the Communist Party emerged as the biggest single Party, with its leader Klement Gottwald as Premier of a coalition government. The Italian elections also showed a great increase in Communist strength and Communists (as in France and Belgium) participated in a government of democratic coalition.

So the *Daily Worker* entered 1947 amid ample signs that the post-war picture was taking definite shape. But the new year had barely passed its third week when the coldest winter spell of modern times froze the country solid until the middle of March. The fuel shortage turned the freeze-up into a national crisis. A great part of industry closed down and millions were temporarily unemployed. Serious work at Farringdon Road became impossible and any hope of the new paper on May 1—or, as it turned out, during 1947 at all—had to be abandoned. Our daily production was a feat of emergency improvisation. The re-imposition of newsprint restrictions from February 12 to March 17 brought the paper temporarily down to its wartime four pages again; and, with the tremendous general dislocation of the freeze-up, something like two-thirds of the extra circulation so gallantly won dwindled away.

The circulation position, plus an advertising decline (by the end of the year the revenue had fallen by something over £300 a week from the 1946 peak) and a steady soar in production costs—newsprint prices rose, printers won a five-day week and wage increases—combined to produce a sharp financial crisis by mid-summer. For the first five months of the year the Fighting Fund had been lagging an average of £600-odd behind its reduced peacetime target of £3,000; and, in sum, as a double-column front page call by William Rust on June 17 indicated, a small favourable balance had been turned into a quarterly deficit of £3,500. Rust announced a number of economy measures, including the dropping of the eight-page Saturday issue which had been introduced at the end of March to encourage the weekend sales that had again become a big feature of the paper's life; and he pronounced the £3,000 Fund target an absolute "must." The readers responded splendidly to the Fund call and circulation rose, though sluggishly.

The climatic accident of the freeze-up had exposed not merely the fuel crisis but a general crisis of Government policy, which the official bleats against "totalitarian" planning (i.e., against any serious planning at all) did nothing to solve. The *Daily Worker* stood out by the responsible and positive treatment it gave to these basic problems. A feature series in March of Britain's crisis and the way out drew contributions from Labour M.P.s and noted orthodox economists like Mrs. Joan Robinson. In June the paper called one of its famous delegate conferences on "Britain's Way Forward." A thousand delegates representing 2,600,000 organised workers packed the Kingsway Hall to hear a powerful and practical opening speech by Arthur Horner for a real Socialist policy and real Socialist planning, and cheered to the echo William Rust's concluding call for a "new declaration of war against the rich and against the Tories" (*Daily Worker,* June 30, 1947). But the Press, notably the *Daily Herald,* boycotted this important conference.

In face of a situation which grew more acute, until in July there appeared the storm signal of a draining away of the dollar reserves, the Government could only retreat and cut. Big Business purred approval of the "austerity" plan introduced by Sir Stafford Cripps in September. Capital reconstruction of industry was axed and the parallel insistence on still further increases in productivity and extension of exports could only presage intensified exploitation of the working class. It was not surprising that the demand for an immediate steel nationalisation Bill received a substantial minority vote at the Southport Trades Union Congress, where also there were loud cheers for delegates who urged that the country should stand on its own feet, not in pawn to America, and where the ultra-reactionary American Federation of Labour speaker was shouted down.

Britain was an integral part of a general picture, which could be summed up as the turn to a new world line-up. In March President Truman demonstratively offered U.S. military and economic aid to Greece and Turkey ("Truman is giving way to the worst imperialists, the atomaniacs and the rest of the wild crew who dream of world domination. And let it not be forgotten that they are dragging Britain down with them" warned our leader on March 13). By May dollar pressure had squeezed the Communist Ministers out of the Governments in France, Italy, Belgium. In

June came the Marshall "plan," for the capitalist reconstruction of Western Europe as an American appanage, and in particular for the reactionary revival of Germany as the economic keystone of the "Western Bloc" which Wall Street needed as its European base for world domination. The Americans, with their British and French satellites, set themselves deliberately to flout Big Four unity and the Potsdam agreement on Germany, to initiate the permanent partitioning of Germany with a puppet West German State under their control; with this aim they cynically and calculatedly broke up the London session of the Council of Foreign Ministers in December, 1947.

Well might William Rust write, for our 18th birthday celebration, an impressive Albert Hall affair on January 4, 1948—"what a year it will be!" For, as he went on to say, "there are now two camps in the world; the imperialist camp and the democratic camp. The *Daily Worker* takes its stand uncompromisingly with the latter. That is the starting point of all our editorial work." And that, further, "puts us in the forefront of the fight for peace" and against the danger of a third world war. The forthright stand of Mr. Vyshinsky at the U.N. General Assembly in the autumn of 1947 on the question of disarmament had already shown very precisely who were the warmongers. During 1948 the warmongering in the West, particularly in America, approached the hysterical. A currency crisis was forced in Berlin and the famous "blockade" and airlift began in June. Warlike measures like Western Union, with its pooling of all armed forces, paved the way for the Atlantic Pact, which sought to provide a cloak of treaty legality for American intervention in the internal affairs of the contracting States should they turn left. Britain again became an American bomber base.

These events gave the *Daily Worker* scope for many big treatments. So did the main developments at home and abroad which reflected the new division of the world. For this division was fundamentally a class division and the sharpening of the class struggle in all capitalist countries became daily more marked. The Labour Government proclaimed a general wage-freeze though the cost of living was ever rising; but at a conference of trade union executives in March the debating honours went to the opposition, who mustered no less than 2,000,000 on a card vote; nor did wage movements cease—they spread to embrace the key sections of industry, miners, railwaymen, engineers, etc. Discontent spread among the workers in the nationalised industries as experience taught them that the new Board was much like the old Capitalist writ large.

A new and sinister feature was the opening of an anti-Communist witch-hunt, both by the State—in the Civil Service—and by the right-wing trade union leadership. The Civil Service purge soon plumbed depths of American absurdity; the initial pretence that it would only be operated where there were security considerations wore mighty thin when it was extended to people in charge of R.A.F. officers' tennis courts or to a secretary of the Minister of Education. The unions concerned were denied the right of representing accused members and the effective direction of operations was entrusted to the anonymous spies of MI5. In the trade union movement, following a preliminary canter by Labour Party secretary Morgan Phillips (later to be named as one of the guests of the scandalous Sydney Stanley*) the T.U.C. General Council reintroduced, in effect, the former "Black Circulars" attempting to ban Communists from holding union office. A stream of protests flowed unceasingly into our columns, which were able to report the substantial failure of these splitting efforts and the number of union posts held, or won, by Communists.

The splitters and witch-hunters were active internationally, too. With the aid of American Federation of Labour representatives the right-wing, headed by Jouhaux, broke away from the French C.G.T. to form the miscalled "Workers' Strength" union grouping. The A.F.L. and C.I.O.—their old enmity dissolved in their new vocation as labour agents of American imperialism abroad—joined with the British General Council to stage a breakaway from the World Federation of Trade Unions, consummated at the Paris Executive meeting of that body in January, 1949, and to organise a new anti-Communist "International." The Italian elections in April provided another object lesson in sabotage of unity. Herbert Morrison made the dispatch of

......................................................

* A fixer and fraudster, Stanley allegedly helped businessmen to bribe ministers and civil servants for favourable treatment. The Lynskey tribunal, which investigated the issue from December 1948 to January 1949, caught the public's attention but resulted in no prosecutions—although one minister, John Belcher, and Bank of England director George Gibson resigned and Stanley fled to Israel.—J.E.

greetings to the pro-unity Socialist Party by a number of Labour M.P.s a major disciplinary issue and secured the expulsion of John Platts-Mills, Finsbury's member. The Americans spent dollars like water to break the Communists, but failed, though the Christian Socialists gained substantially; it was noticeable that the agency message reporting that the Americans had spent $5,000,000 to fix the elections, though available to all newspapers, was printed only in the *Daily Worker* (April 22).

In one vital quarter world reaction suffered a setback of the first order. The attempt was made to drag Czechoslovakia into the Marshall net, starting with the break-up of the existing National Front Government (i.e., ousting the Communists) and preparing if necessary to go to the length of a right-wing putsch. But the unity of the Czech working class was unbreakable and the Communist Party, under the inspired leadership of Gottwald, proved more than equal to the occasion. The February days marked much more than the utter rout of the plotters; they brought about one of history's very rare constitutional and bloodless revolutions. Not that the envenomed howls of the thwarted Anglo-American reactionaries were any less; they had permanently lost the most highly industrialised and advanced country of Central Europe to the Communist-led, Socialism-building, People's Democracies. The subsequent defection of the Tito régime in Yugoslavia was a poor sort of consolation prize. We were fortunate in having a colourful eyewitness Prague story from Alan Winnington en route for China and the history-changing triumphs of the People's Liberation armies.

Many were the other centres of conflict calling for news treat-ment and comment. The evacuation of Palestine finally forced on Britain unleashed the Jewish-Arab war in May. Derek Kartun did a first-rate job as a front-line reporter and brought our readers real understanding of the complex situation out of which arose the new State of Israel, utterly confounding Mr. Bevin and his pro-Arab "experts" by the crushing military defeat it inflicted on the Arab States leagued against it. In Greece the handful of hunted men who had taken to the mountains two years before were now the disciplined army of a provisional Government, beating off the heaviest American-aided offensives and taking frequent offensive action themselves. We managed to get Evdos Joannides, well-known Cypriot Communist journalist, through to the remote fastnesses of Free Greece; the noble and heroic story he had to tell, in a series beginning with the first interview with General Markos—then C.-in-C.—to appear in a British newspaper (*Daily Worker,* June 12, 1948), ranks as one of our greatest beats in the field of foreign correspondence. In Malaya a colonial war of exceptional brutality, with wholesale village-burnings and the like, was launched against the former leaders of the liberation fight against the Japanese whom repression had driven to the jungle; single-handed the *Daily Worker* told the truth about Malaya in the face of a constant and virulent Press campaign against "bandits and terrorists." In India the Nehru-Patel Government out-Britished the British in repression of the Communists, the trade unions and all progressive mass move-ments; there was nothing to restrain them after Gandhi fell on

January 30 to the bullets of a Hindu chauvinist assassin—just as he was shaking off his traditional anti-Communism (an ugly parallel with the similar assassination of Burma's General Aung San*).

In retrospect, the life of the paper during the first ten months of 1948 seems like the prehistory of the great change, the new *Daily Worker* of November 1. But that firm date was not finally announced until June 19, when the Editor told readers that the price of the new paper would have to be 1½d., and called on them for the £44,000 needed to bring the P.P.P.S. capital up to the required quarter of a million—£30,000 of it by the launching date. Already we had two remarkable examples of response to a real mobilisation of our supporters for circulation. Two eight-page issues, one in February for the Communist Manifesto centenary (the historic document was textually reprinted), and one for May Day ran to sales of 230,000 and 251,000—an absolute record—respectively. The institution of a "Meet the Editor" reception hour at the office on Tuesday evenings proved a popular and instructive innovation.

It was of good augury that a peace conference initiated by the paper, with the participation of the National Peace Council, proved the most imposing gathering of the kind in our whole history. Labour movement militants and middle-class pacifists united at the Friends' Meeting House on July 17 in a representation of no less than 3,449,000. The Dean of Canterbury

........................................................

* Father of the jailed pro-democracy leader Aung San Suu Kyi.—J.E.

and Dr. Alex Wood (the Peace Council's chairman) were the principal speakers. Characteristically our leading article of July 20 had to note—

"The great peace conference called by the *Daily Worker* was largely boycotted by the Press and B.B.C. This is, indeed, an example of how the freedom of the Press (Fleet Street model) works in the selection and suppression of news. The smallest items from Berlin make headlines. The story of a British official who was detained in Germany by the Russians for three days gets a front page column. But the greatest mass peace conference ever held in Britain gets hardly a mention."*

........................................

* Sharp exposure of the Millionaire Press and its methods was a speciality of William Rust's. Hostile elements among Fleet Street journalists seized on a later withering leader ("Dunghill Ethics," November 5, 1948) to attack Rust in the Central London branch of the N.U.J., of which he was a member; and he had prepared one of the fighting speeches of his lifetime for a special meeting of the branch on this issue, scheduled for the day he died. Similarly when he led the paper's representatives to give evidence before the Royal Commission on the Press he dealt mercilessly with those reactionary Commissioners who were more interested in attacking the *Daily Worker* than in exposing the millionaire monopolists, as their subsequent Report showed (paras. 445-448). That Report, by abstracting a question and answer from its context, suggested that Rust and the *Daily Worker* were not interested in accuracy; actually, there was a pedantic and hair-splitting attack launched by the right-wing publicist, R.C.K. Ensor, over our treatment of some Greek news and a number of peppery exchanges over accuracy, "material points" and the like. Rust summed up with the words: "Anybody with a serious interest in the truth would not try to split hairs over the matter that our statement gave the facts that are going on in Greece at the present time" (Minutes of

As the summer passed everything speeded up for our D-Day. There were anxieties in plenty. While the readers' rally to the appeal for capital was magnificent (before November 1 we got not the £30,000 called for, but more than £35,000), the advertising decline had become a slump; weekly revenue was less than a third of what it had been at the peak, two years before. It was therefore decided that the new paper would have to forego its Late London edition (the economy proved a false one and a month after November 1 a modified Late London edition was resumed).

On Saturday, October 30, our last Swinton Street small-size paper appeared, with a rousing front-page lead by the Editor reiterating the main points of the new full-size four-pager, giving 20 per cent. more space than the old six pages and having a technical base the last word in modernity. That Saturday was no day of rest for our staff. Everyone turned up, the Editor included, to help in moving the office furniture, files and fittings. It was all very dirty and very lively. The present writer remembers best the last lurching van journey, with the night printer and himself

......................................

Evidence, Day 21, Q. 6999). The paper also submitted a detailed reply to the Commission's questionnaire to all papers; it was the one fundamental treatment of the Press, its character and rôle, in the volume of Memoranda of Evidence, No. 3 (pp. 152-155). Our document made, among other basic points, the vital one that "accuracy in a newspaper is not only a matter of the correctness of the news it carries but of the accuracy with which the newspaper as a whole reflects the significant news of the day." This was reproduced in the Commission's Report, apparently with approval (para. 369).

nursing the precious feature page for the new paper's first issue, already set and made up.

Sunday, October 31, was The Day for us. Full of technical tribulations, as such days always are in the life of any newspaper, an overwhelming compensation was at hand. Half our linotypes jibbed at the post—we had to run the machines remaining at the old plant for weeks, as it turned out—we were late on edition and missed trains; but what were tribulations when you had torchlight with them? A great demonstration had assembled during the afternoon on Clerkenwell Green, just round the corner from No. 75. They heard Harry Pollitt acclaim the "greatest and proudest day" in the paper's history. Then, as evening fell, the demonstrators, estimated at 20,000, marched in torchlight procession to our building, entirely blocking Farringdon Road and stopping all traffic.

We were surrounded by a surging sea of supporters whose cheers rolled and echoed as the rhythmic beat-beat-beat of the superb Goss machine told that the paper was at last running. When William Rust appeared with the first two copies off he was able to auction them for no less than £45 apiece; and then the roaring crowd seized him and bore him shoulder-high round the block, the torches palely flickering in the white brilliance of our window lights. It was undoubtedly the highest of all high spots in the life of the *Daily Worker,* that demonstration, and it deeply moved all those of us, in the edition battle line, who rushed from desk and stone and machine to look out on it; it deeply moved, too, the many representatives of the Communist

Press in other countries who had come to greet us, notably France's beloved veteran Marcel Cachin.

Next day, proud in the knowledge that circulation had bounded up nearly 20 per cent., that even the ranks of Fleet Street could scarce forbear to cheer, we were prouder still of the simple telegram from the famous Dorset village of Tolpuddle which spoke for all our supporters. Signed by George Loveless, a descendant of the martyrs of 1834, it read: "Today is a proud day for us all. This is what our ancestors fought for. Long live the People's Paper!"

This history ought to have finished on that note; but fate willed otherwise. With the new paper only three months old it suffered its cruellest and most searching blow. On February 3, 1949, its Editor, William Rust, collapsed and died of a stroke. His closest associates on the paper are still stunned by the blow as these lines are written, six months later. But the tributes that poured in last February from all over the movement and all over the world were also tributes to the power of the paper that Bill Rust and his Party had built from the bottom up. The dignified demonstration of 5,000 that made his funeral so profoundly impressive was a mass dedication to the cause voiced and led by the *Daily Worker* as well as a last salute to the man whom his old comrade and successor, J.R. Campbell, so rightly called "the greatest Editor in British working-class history." Bill Rust made his own monument if any man ever did; these pages have told its story; and it is raised anew to him every day.

# Index

## A

Africa, war in  187, 211, 213
Air-raids  149, 166-7, 171, 185-6, 229
Allison, George  43, 158, 184, 202
Arnot, R. Page  15, 62, 164
Asten, Fred  191
Atomic bomb  149, 242-3
Attlee, Clement  73-4, 76, 125, 241-2

## B

Baldwin, Stanley (Earl)  39, 68, 73, 82, 90-2
Bassett, Archie  191
Beaverbrook, Lord  192, 196, 212
Belgium  160, 233, 250, 252
Bevan, Aneurin  35, 76, 121, 178, 210
Beveridge Report  209, 222
Bevin, Ernest  55-7, 64, 156, 159, 162, 242-4, 249, 257
Big Three
  Potsdam  242, 253
  Teheran  218
  Yalta  226, 230
Bishop, Reg  59
Bradley, Ben  63, 164

## C

Campbell, J.R.  203, 262

Canterbury, Dean of  208

Chamberlain, Neville  29, 98-103, 105-15, 120-6, 143, 145-8, 151, 153, 161, 169

China  45, 49, 91, 203, 256

Churchill, Winston  76, 96, 99, 110, 125, 144, 161, 178, 187, 189, 193-4, 196,
     211, 213, 215, 218, 224, 228-34, 240-5, 249

Citrine, Lord (Sir Walter)  66, 87, 89-90, 109, 158-9, 169, 217-8, 234

Cockburn, Claud—*see Pitcairn, Frank*

Co-operative Movement  104, 199, 239

Communist International  18-21, 51, 53-4, 61, 63, 66, 220

Communist parties
  Belgium  250, 252
  Britain  15-18, 23, 48, 51, 54, 61, 65-6, 69, 76, 85, 87, 103, 109, 120, 122,
     125, 144, 146-7, 153, 163, 174, 176, 188, 190, 197, 202, 206, 211, 213-14,
     220-1, 241, 245, 247
  Czechoslovakia  107, 250, 256
  France  162, 224, 243, 250, 252
  Germany  35, 49, 53, 62, 203
  Greece  233, 249
  India  257
  Italy  250, 252, 256
  Soviet Union  123

Conservative Party  20, 39, 69, 90, 95, 98, 109, 148, 181, 221, 228, 240-1,
     245

Cripps, Sir Stafford  33, 62, 76, 78-9, 88, 95, 120-2, 147, 149, 187, 248, 250,
     252

Czechoslovakia  29, 92, 97, 103-6, 108, 110, 112-6, 122-3, 145, 250, 256

# D

Daily Express  28, 54, 228, 241

Daily Herald  16-7, 26, 28, 58, 77, 90-1, 93-4, 106, 109, 193, 196, 240, 252

Daily Mail  29-30, 36, 57, 59, 77, 97-8, 152, 155

Daily Mirror  29, 77, 93, 178, 182, 196, 208

Daily Worker
  "specials"  188, 191
  advertising  26-7, 44, 78, 116-7, 205, 246, 250, 260

blitzed  167-8, 185, 186
circulation  24, 26, 33, 37, 44-5, 65, 78, 118, 126, 191, 205-6, 245, 250-1,
    258, 262
conferences  208, 221, 238-9, 251-2, 258-9
court cases  31-2, 41-4, 46-7, 55-7, 79, 87-9, 158-9
editorial board  56, 81, 163-4, 176, 180, 182, 186, 189, 195, 200, 207-8,
    237-8
fighting fund  29, 41, 44-5, 54, 57, 78, 116-8, 158, 160, 165, 170, 184, 202,
    239, 251
leagues  158, 184, 199-200
People's Press Printing Society  239-40, 245, 258
plants
    Cayton Street  64, 78-9, 86, 168, 174, 185-6
    Farringdon Road  237, 245-7, 250, 260-1
    Swinton Street  201-2, 204, 260
    Utopia Press  24-5, 40, 43, 46-7, 55, 64
    police and  31, 40-44, 65, 164, 174, 179, 180, 185
    Scottish printing  169-170
    sport  30, 245
    war correspondent ban  228-9
    wholesalers' boycott  22-4, 65, 205
Dimitrov, Georgi  53, 62-3
Dutt, R. Palme  37, 99, 116, 250


# E

Eden, Anthony  96, 98-103, 145, 195, 198, 212, 230, 234
Engineers  188, 192, 219


# F

Fascism  58, 61, 66-7, 71, 75-6, 85, 90, 93-5, 119-120, 125-6, 148-9, 152, 154,
    179, 190, 195, 214, 223, 232, 234-5, 249
Finland  123, 145, 156-7
France  53, 90-91, 94, 97, 104, 107, 109, 112, 114-5, 123-4, 126, 143-4, 148-9,
    153, 155, 160, 162-3, 209, 224, 229, 233, 243, 250, 252
Friell, Jimmy—*see Gabriel*

# G

Gabriel (cartoonist) 30, 80, 82, 100
Gallacher, William 15, 30, 69, 114, 122, 178-9, 241
General Elections
  1931 37, 44
  1935 68-9
  1945 240-1
Germany 50, 52-3, 58, 68, 74, 90-1, 95, 98, 108, 110, 114, 123-4, 126, 145-6,
    148-9, 194, 204, 212, 214, 218, 230-2, 242, 253, 259
Gibson, George 190, 255
Greece 187, 232-4, 249, 252, 257, 259

# H

Haldane, J.B.S. 80-1, 149-50, 161-2, 164, 176, 180, 183, 189, 243
Hannington, Wal 47
Hitler, Adolf 29, 49, 52, 57-8, 68, 71, 73, 75, 90-91, 93-6, 98-100, 102-3, 105-
    16, 122, 146-8, 162, 187, 209, 213-14, 228-9, 232, 234
Holmes, Walter 15, 16, 30, 45-6, 67, 119, 185, 249
Horner, Arthur 47, 49, 208, 219, 248, 251
Housing 223, 248
Hutt, Allen 16, 64, 197, 203

# I

Independent Labour Party 61, 76, 113
India 21, 35, 63, 154, 173, 195, 207, 209, 250, 257
Italy 67, 74, 90, 145, 166, 214-16, 252

# J

Japan 45, 49, 90-1, 105, 166, 195, 242-3, 257

# K

Kartun, Derek 246, 257
Kemsley, Lord 97-8, 148, 159, 171, 209, 222

# L

Labour Government
　1931　37-9
　1945　241-2, 244-5, 247-9
Labour Party　26, 37-40, 54, 66, 76, 83, 92, 99, 102-3, 120-1, 149, 165, 175,
　　　195, 197, 199-200, 220-1, 240-1, 247
Lenin　18, 71, 75, 226
Lloyd George, David　106, 144, 197

# M

MacEwen, Malcolm　244
Mann, Tom　41, 47-8
Maro (cartoonist)　30, 60-61, 72
Miners　181, 190, 192, 208, 219-20, 254
Molotov, V.M.　144, 198, 249
Montagu, Ivor　203, 249
Morrison, Herbert　33, 122, 143, 162, 167-9, 171, 173-83, 185-6, 190, 195, 197-
　　　200, 205, 220, 227, 255
Mosley, Oswald　35-8, 84, 86-7, 194, 227, 244
Mussolini, Benito　67, 71, 73, 99-100, 102, 106, 113, 122, 126, 214-5

# N

News Chronicle　75, 109, 181-2, 191, 228

# O

O'Casey, Sean　164
Owen, Jack　164

# P

Papworth, A.F.　56-7, 208, 221, 234
Pateman, Fred　216, 246
Paterson, Frank　15, 31-2, 42
People's Convention　168, 171-3

Piratin, Phil 241
Pitcairn, Frank 70, 72, 74-5, 105, 108, 172-3, 183, 224
Poland 123, 125-6, 143, 146, 149, 152, 225-6
Pollitt, Harry 23, 54-5, 64, 69, 73, 92, 103, 118, 190, 213-4, 261
Press
  capitalist 16-17, 26-9, 96-8, 256-7, 259-60
  Royal Commission on 15, 27-8, 259-60
Pritt, D.N. 62, 155, 158, 165, 172

# R

Reynolds News 30, 104, 155, 177, 197, 203
Roosevelt, President 210, 218, 230, 235
Rowney, W.D.—*see Maro*
Rust, William 15-16, 31-2, 50-1, 72-3, 104, 158, 161, 168, 181, 183, 185, 190-1, 204, 206, 228, 238, 240, 244, 250-3, 259, 261-2

# S

Second Front 190, 193-9, 207-18, 223, 229-30
Shaw, George Bernard 161, 183, 239
Shepherd, W.G. 15, 43, 170, 246
Soviet Union 35, 49-50, 57-9, 63, 66-8, 90, 92-5, 107, 109, 112, 114-5, 123-6, 143-4, 146-7, 151, 154-7, 173, 176, 183, 187, 189-90, 198, 210, 218, 225-6, 231-2, 242-3
Spain 51, 53, 60, 71-5, 91, 96, 100, 102-5, 116, 120-1, 145, 204, 232
Stalin, Joseph 52, 123-4, 126, 148, 187, 194, 211, 213-4, 217-8, 226, 230-1
Stalingrad, Battle of 198-9, 209-11, 213, 217
Sunday Express 210

# T

Tapsell, Walter 72-3
Templewood, Lord (Sir S. Hoare) 28-9, 67, 87, 97, 211, 214, 223-4
The Times 16-7, 19-20, 33, 67, 70, 77, 81, 93, 96, 108, 156, 162, 183, 195, 212, 226, 233, 243
Tories—*see Conservatives*

Trades Union Congress  57, 66, 102, 113, 153, 158-9, 169, 190, 194, 196, 199-
    200, 210, 216-7, 221-2, 229, 234, 248, 252, 255
Truman, President  249, 252

# U

Unemployed  19, 34, 38-9, 46, 48, 50, 66, 69, 95, 119-20, 250
Unions
    A.U.B.T.W.  172
    Amalgamated Engineering Union (A.E.U.)  46, 164-5, 189, 194, 208, 219,
        221
    Associated Society of Locomotive Engineers and Firemen  172
    B.I.S.A.K.T.A.  201
    National Union of Distributive and Allied Workers  104
    National Union of Journalists (N.U.J.)  169, 188, 259
    National Union of Mineworkers  169, 208, 248
    National Union of Railwaymen (N.U.R.)  82, 165, 176, 220
    Natsopa  180
    Shop Assistants' Union  104
    Transport and General Workers' Union  156, 208, 210, 217
United States  34, 50, 124, 166, 195-6, 212-4, 216, 223-4, 235, 242, 248, 252

# W

Webb, Beatrice  212
Witch-hunt  254-6
World Federation of Trade Unions  222, 255

# Y

Yugoslavia  187, 225, 256

Lightning Source UK Ltd.
Milton Keynes UK
17 May 2010

154319UK00001B/2/P

9 780954 147310